Prophetic Verse

PROPHETIC VERSE

Including "The Gods of the Copybook Headings"

❖ RUDYARD KIPLING ❖

STONEWELL PRESS

Cover design: Nathaniel J. Parry

ISBN 978–1–62730–110–7

Published by Stonewell Press
Salt Lake City, UT
stonewellpress.com

Contents

III   Life and Death   61

IV Government and Politics   105

PREFACE

A prophet is a truth-teller, one who bears testimony of that which his fellows need to hear.

A prophet is one who speaks for all ages—whose truths do not tarnish or grow out of date every few years.

In some ways, Rudyard Kipling (1865–1936) regarded himself as a prophet.[1] The content and biblical language of many of his poems support that view. They speak of a God-centered universe, on that is governed by divine law. They speak truth—often hard truth—that strikes to the heart of the challenges of the twenty-first century: war, destruction, greed, hatred, contempt for human life. Some of his writings speak of the goodness of the Creator and of His power to help us in a difficult world. Some warn against the sins of pride and covetousness, selfishness, and callousness. And some give instructions about how to make one's way through the befuddling labyrinth of life.

Kipling himself felt the weight of a prophetic calling. "I am daily and nightly perplexed with my own responsibilities before God," he wrote to a friend in 1897.[2]

What he saw in himself others also saw in him.

His sister, Alice Fleming, said a year after his death, "Critics to-day are apt to forget that Rudyard Kipling felt from the beginning that the word of the Lord was laid upon him, and he had to do that for which he was sent."[3]

In discussing the prophetic nature of the title poem to this collection, "The Gods of the Copybook Headings," Kipling scholar Gerard E. Fox

---

1. For an in-depth discussion of Kipling as prophet, see Esther Marian Greenwell Smith, *The Prophetic Qualities of Rudyard Kipling's Work,* PhD dissertation (Gainesville, Florida: University of Florida, 1972).

2. C. E. Carrington, *The Life of Rudyard Kipling* (Garden City, New York: Doubleday & Company, 1955), 248.

3. Alice Fleming, "The Annual Luncheon," *The Kipling Journal,* June 1937, 63.

said, "When the need arises, there has always appeared a Prophet or Seer able to tell the people the truth, and, as indicated above, I look upon Mr. Kipling as one of these, and the wonder is that he has not yet been stoned for his pains."[4] Twenty years later, after Kipling had been dead for a decade, Fox continued the theme, calling him "a Seer, a Prophet, a Visionary, with all his realism."[5]

Another Kipling devotee, A. E. G. Cornwell, colorfully described the poet as "Loving his country and countrymen, with a proud and passionate love, yet flaying them with whips of scorpions, like a prophet of old, when he thinks they are not living up to the sturdy traditions passed on by their rough forefathers."[6]

Cornwell then quoted another author who, "in many a tight place, when everything seemed hopeless, . . . turned to Kipling for help and comfort as another man would 'turn to his Bible.'" And yet another said of Kipling, "He himself has not the faintest idea of the help he has been to thousands. . . . He speaks God's messages in language so many can understand."[7]

In a tribute offered a few months after Kipling's death, his friend Lionel Dunsterville called him a "poet and prophet for all the human race."[8]

No less a poet and critic than T. S. Eliot held a similar view. "Kipling was something rarer than a philosopher, he was a prophet," Eliot wrote. "He had a gift for prophecy."[9] Kipling had "a queer gift of second sight," Eliot observed, "of transmitting messages from elsewhere, a gift so disconcerting when we are made aware of it that thenceforth we are never sure when it is *not* present."[10]

A more recent Kipling scholar wrote:

---

4. Gerard E. Fox, "The Poet as Prophet," *The Kipling Journal,* March 1927, 29-30. In that same essay, Fox said even more plainly: "I believe that to-day we possess a true Prophet in Mr. Rudyard Kipling."

5. Gerard E. Fox, "Rudyard Kipling the Tribal Singer," *The Kipling Journal,* July 1947, 8.

6. A. E. G. Cornwell, "The Apostle of Work and Service," *The Kipling Journal,* December 1938, 131.

7. A. E. G. Cornwell, "The Apostle of Work and Service," *The Kipling Journal,* December 1938, 131-32.

8. L. C. Dunsterville, "Message to the English Speaking Union," *The Kipling Journal,* September 1936, 80.

9. T. S. Eliot, "The Unfading Genius of Rudyard Kipling," *The Kipling Journal,* March 1959, 12.

10. T. S. Eliot, *A Choice of Kipling's Verse* (New York: Charles Scribner's Sons, 1943), 22.

Kipling, seen through his work, fulfills a prophetic role, from the agony of lonely commitment to the authority of an inspired message. Furthermore, he uses the language and material of the Bible and other religious resources as an essential idiom of his art, and he establishes the framework for his artistic themes on a God-oriented structure of Divine Law for the universe, Divine Love for all creatures, Divine Concern with all Reality, and Divine Source for all Truth. . . .

The term *prophetic* is used, then, in its Scriptural sense: the work of men under divine mandate who look at their world with spiritually heightened insight and present messages of judgment and mercy.[11]

The evidence is clear, she continued, "that Kipling so understood his work, as a vocation under God, as a prophetic mandate." His was the theme shared by "all Judeo-Christian prophets": "that the Supreme Being is as real as, if not more real than the phenomena men call reality," and that He gave meaning and vitality to life. "It is this concept that Kipling was convinced God had called him to reiterate in modes that would reach an audience no longer (to some extent never) reached by strictly religious teaching."[12]

"His personal creed . . . was deeply reverent," a friend added. "Rudyard Kipling had a religion and it dominated his life."[13]

In his poem "Non Nobis Domine," published in 1934, Kipling expressed his tender, respectful feelings toward God:

"O Power by Whom we live—
Creator, Judge, and Friend,
Upholdingly forgive
Nor fail us at the end. . . ."

The accuracy of Kipling's warnings was so high that in 1919 one critic published an article titled "The Remarkable Rightness of Rudyard Kipling"—in no less an outlet than *Atlantic* magazine. Kipling was

---

11. Esther Marian Greenwell Smith, *The Prophetic Qualities of Rudyard Kipling's Work*, PhD dissertation (Gainesville, Florida: University of Florida, 1972), vii-viii.

12. Esther Marian Greenwell Smith, *The Prophetic Qualities of Rudyard Kipling's Work*, PhD dissertation (Gainesville, Florida: University of Florida, 1972), vii-viii.

13. Lucille Russell Carpenter, *Rudyard Kipling: A Friendly Profile* (Chicago: Argus Books, 1942), 66.

"right," she said, "because time has sustained him against scoffers." His rightness was "remarkable," she continued, "because no one originally expected that kind of rightness from him."[14]

Kipling was the first Englishman to be awarded a Nobel Prize for Literature, which he received just over a century ago. (He received the award in 1907, at age forty-two—and still is the youngest person so honored.) But many of his poems are timeless, as relevant today as they were then. He was a keen observer of human nature—and of his times—which were much like our times: government leaders who were inept or corrupt or both, foreign conflicts that never seemed to end (or simply cropped up in other places), a populace who had largely forgotten God, and a general confusion about what was right and what was wrong.

To some degree, Kipling has fallen out of favor. Even during his lifetime one writer said,

> There has been more than one reason . . . for the waning of Kipling's popularity. . . . He has had an unlucky trick of seeing ahead. . . . But there are other causes more insidious and more potent. He stands . . . for a lot of . . . outdated things: pious attachment to the soil; romantic love, enduring, clean outside and in; the beauty of childhood and the bitterer beauty of parenthood; patriotism unshrinking; and unashamed; loathing of the mob and the mob's madness and meanness; the continuity of the English political tradition, from Magna Charta down; religious toleration.[15]

Some of Kipling's work is dated, expressive of a sensibility that is sometimes disturbing, sometimes too reflective of a by-gone culture, sometimes politically incorrect by our standards. All that is to be expected from a writer whose work was mostly completed nearly a century ago. Yet he has so much to offer a troubled and stumbling world that our loss would be very great indeed were we to forget this remarkable poet-prophet, Rudyard Kipling, who spoke for all times.

J.A.P.
April 2015

---

14. Katharine Fullerton Gerould, "The Remarkable Rightness of Rudyard Kipling," *The Atlantic,* Jan. 1919.
15. Katharine Fullerton Gerould, "The Remarkable Rightness of Rudyard Kipling," *The Atlantic,* Jan. 1919.

Part I

PROPHETIC VERSE

THE GODS OF THE COPYBOOK HEADINGS

As I pass through my incarnations in every age and race,
I make my proper protestations to the Gods of the Market-Place.
Peering through reverent fingers I watch them flourish and fall.
And the Gods of the Copybook Headings,[1] I notice, outlast them all.

We were living in trees when they met us. They showed us each in turn,
That water would certainly wet us, as Fire would certainly burn:
But we found them lacking in Uplift, Vision, and Breadth of Mind,
So we left them to teach the Gorillas while we followed the March
of Mankind.

We moved as the Spirit listed. *They* never altered their pace,
Being neither cloud nor wind-borne like the Gods of the Market-Place;
But they always caught up with our progress, and presently word
would come
That a tribe had been wiped off its icefield, or the lights had gone
out in Rome.

With the Hopes that our World is built on they were utterly out of touch.
They denied that the Moon was Stilton; they denied she was even
Dutch.[2]
They denied that Wishes were Horses; they denied that a Pig had Wings.
So we worshiped the Gods of the Market Who promised these beautiful
things.

---

1. Copybook headings were wise maxims printed at the top of students' copybook pages in the nineteenth century. The students learned both penmanship and moral principles by copying the headings again and again on the page beneath the heading. The copybook headings represent the foundational principles of a moral life, which are contrasted with the trendy, ephemeral ideas of the "Gods of the Market-Place."
2. Stilton is an expensive form of cheese, and Dutch cheeses come in many varieties.

When the Cambrian[3] measures were forming, They promised perpetual
  peace.
They swore, if we gave them our weapons, that the wars of the tribes
  would cease.
But when we disarmed They sold us and delivered us bound to our foe,
And the Gods of the Copybook Headings said: *"Stick to the Devil you
  know."*

On the first Feminian[4] Sandstones we were promised the Fuller Life
(Which started by loving our neighbor and ended by loving his wife)
Till our women had no more children and the men lost reason and faith,
And the Gods of the Copybook Headings said: *"The Wages of Sin is
  Death!"*

In the Carboniferous[5] Epoch we were promised abundance for all,
By robbing selective Peter to pay for collective Paul;
But, though we had plenty of money, there was nothing our money
  could buy,
And the Gods of the Copybook Headings said: *"If you don't work you
  die."*

Then the Gods of the Market tumbled, and their smooth-tongued
  wizards withdrew,
And the hearts of the meanest were humbled and began to believe
  it was true
That All is not Gold that Glitters, and Two and Two make Four—
And the Gods of the Copybook Headings limped up to explain it once
  more.

***

As it will be in the future, it was at the birth of Man—
There are only four things certain since Social Progress began:—
That the Dog returns to his Vomit and the Sow returns to her mire,
And the burnt Fool's bandaged finger goes wabbling back to the Fire;

---

3. Cambrian refers to an early geological period. Symbolically, it has reference to
Wales, the Latin name of which is *Cambria*. Lloyd George, a Welshman, was Great
Britain's prime minister for much of World War I. He helped negotiate the Treaty of
Versailles of 1919, which ended the war but also required Britain and its allies to begin
to disarm themselves.
   4. This is a made-up geological term that refers to the emancipation of women.
   5. A geological term that refers to the formation of coal. In the poem, coal miners
represent the power of the trade unions.

And that after this is accomplished, and the brave new world begins
When all men are paid for existing and no man must pay for his sins,
As surely as Water will wet us, as surely as Fire will burn,
The Gods of the Copybook Headings with terror and slaughter return!

"BEFORE A MIDNIGHT BREAKS IN STORM"

Before a midnight breaks in storm,
  Or herded sea in wrath,
Ye know what wavering gusts inform
  The greater tempest's path;
    Till the loosed wind
    Drive all from mind,
Except Distress, which, so will prophets cry,
O'ercame them, houseless, from the unhinting sky.

Ere rivers league against the land
  In piratry of flood,
Ye know what waters steal and stand
  Where seldom water stood.
    Yet who will note,
    Till fields afloat,
And washen carcass and the returning well,
Trumpet what these poor heralds strove to tell?

Ye know who use the Crystal Ball
  (To peer by stealth on Doom),
The Shade that, shaping first of all,
  Prepares an empty room.
    Then doth It pass
    Like breath from glass,
But, on the extorted Vision bowed intent,
No man considers why It came or went.

Before the years reborn behold
   Themselves with stranger eye,
And the sport-making Gods of old,
    Like Samson slaying, die,
      Many shall hear
      The all-pregnant sphere,
Bow to the birth and sweat, but—speech denied—
Sit dumb or—dealt in part—fall weak and wide.

Yet instant to fore-shadowed need
   The eternal balance swings;
That winged men the Fates may breed
    So soon as Fate hath wings.
      These shall possess
      Our littleness,
And in the imperial task (as worthy) lay
Up our lives' all to piece one giant Day.

THE DYKES

We have no heart for the fishing—we have no hand for the oar—
All that our fathers taught us of old pleases us now no more;
All that our own hearts bid us believe we doubt where we do not deny—
There is no proof[1] in the bread we eat or rest in the toil we ply.

Look you, our foreshore stretches far through sea-gate, dyke and
    groin—
Made land all, that our fathers made, where the flats and the fairway[2]
    join.
They forced the sea a sea-league back. They died, and their work
    stood fast.
We were born to peace in the lee of the dykes, but the time of our
    peace is past.

Far off, the full tide clambers and slips, mouthing and testing all,
Nipping the flanks of the water-gates, baying along the wall;
Turning the shingle, returning the shingle, changing the set of the
    sand . . .
We are too far from the beach, men say, to know how the outworks
    stand.

So we come down, uneasy, to look, uneasily pacing the beach.
These are the dykes our fathers made: we have never known a breach.
Time and again has the gale blown by and we were not afraid;
Now we come only to look at the dykes—at the dykes our fathers made.

---

1. Leaven.
2. Navigable channel.

O'er the marsh where the homesteads cower apart the harried
    sunlight flies,
Shifts and considers, wanes and recovers, scatters and sickens
    and dies—
An evil ember bedded in ash—a spark blown west by wind . . .
We are surrendered to night and the sea—the gale and the tide behind!

At the bridge of the lower saltings[3] the cattle gather and blare,
Roused by the feet of running men, dazed by the lantern glare.
Unbar and let them away for their lives—the levels drown as they stand,
Where the flood-wash forces the sluices aback and the ditches deliver
    inland.

Ninefold deep to the top of the dykes the galloping breakers stride,
And their overcarried spray is a sea—a sea of the landward side.
Coming, like stallions they paw with their hooves, going they snatch
    with their teeth,
Till the bents and the furze and the sand are dragged out, and the
    old-time hurdles beneath.[4]

Bid men gather fuel for fire, the tar, the oil and tow—
Flame we shall need, not smoke, in the dark if the riddled seabanks go.
Bid the ringers watch in the tower (who know how the dawn shall
    prove?)
Each with his rope between his feet and the trembling bells above.

Now we can only wait till the day, wait and apportion our shame.
These are the dykes our fathers left, but we would not look to the same.
Time and again were we warned of the dykes, time and again we
    delayed:
Now, it may fall, we have slain our sons, as our fathers we have
    betrayed.

***

Walking along the wreck of the dykes, watching the work of the seas!
These were the dykes our fathers made to our great profit and ease.
But the peace is gone and the profit is gone, with the old sure days
    withdrawn . . .
That our own houses show as strange when we come back in the dawn!

---

3. Low inland pastures that sometimes have brackish water.
4. The terminology in this line refers to aspects of constructing a dyke.

A RECANTATION (EXCERPT)

What boots it on the Gods to call?
  Since, answered or unheard,
We perish with the Gods and all
  Things made—except the Word. . . .

Yet they who use the Word assigned,
  To hearten and make whole,
Not less than Gods have served mankind,
  Though vultures rend their soul.

"THE CITY OF BRASS"

"Here was a people whom after their works
thou shalt see wept over for their lost dominion:
and in this palace is the last information
respecting lords collected in the dust."
         —The Arabian Nights

In a land that the sand overlays—the ways to her gates are untrod—
A multitude ended their days whose gates were made splendid by God,
Till they grew drunk and were smitten with madness and went to their fall,
And of these is a story written: but Allah Alone knoweth all!

When the wine stirred in their heart their bosoms dilated.
They rose to suppose themselves kings over all things created—
To decree a new earth at a birth without labour or sorrow—
To declare: "We prepare it today and inherit tomorrow."
They chose themselves prophets and priests of minute understanding,
Men swift to see done, and outrun, their extremest commanding—
Of the tribe which describe with a jibe the perversions of Justice—
Panders avowed to the crowd whatsoever its lust is.

Swiftly these pulled down the walls that their fathers had made them—
The impregnable ramparts of old, they razed and relaid them
As playgrounds of pleasure and leisure, with limitless entries,
And havens of rest for the wastrels where once walked the sentries;
And because there was need of more pay for the shouters and marchers,
They disbanded in face of their foemen their yeomen and archers.
They replied to their well-wishers' fears—to their enemies' laughter,
Saying: "Peace! We have fashioned a God Which shall save us hereafter.
We ascribe all dominion to man in his factions conferring,
And have given to numbers the Name of the Wisdom unerring."

11

They said: "Who has hate in his soul? Who has envied his neighbour?
Let him arise and control both that man and his labour."
They said: "Who is eaten by sloth? Whose unthrift has destroyed him?
He shall levy a tribute from all because none have employed him."
They said: "Who hath toiled, who hath striven, and gathered
    possession?
Let him be spoiled. He hath given full proof of transgression."
They said: "Who is irked by the Law? *Though we may not remove it.
If he lend us his aid in this raid, we will set him above it!"*
So the robber did judgment again upon such as displeased him,
The slayer, too, boasted his slain, and the judges released him.

As for their kinsmen far off, on the skirts of the nation,
They harried all earth to make sure none escaped reprobation.
They awakened unrest for a jest in their newly-won borders,
And jeered at the blood of their brethren betrayed by their orders.
They instructed the ruled to rebel, their rulers to aid them;
And, since such as obeyed them not fell, their Viceroys obeyed them.
When the riotous set them at naught they said: "Praise the upheaval!
For the show and the world and the thought of Dominion is evil!"

They unwound and flung from them with rage, as a rag that defied
    them,
The imperial gains of the age which their forefathers piled them.
They ran panting in haste to lay waste and embitter for ever
The wellsprings of Wisdom and Strength which are Faith and
    Endeavour.
They nosed out and digged up and dragged forth and exposed to
    derision
All doctrine of purpose and worth and restraint and prevision:
And it ceased, and God granted them all things for which they had
    striven,
And the heart of a beast in the place of a man's heart was given. . . .

***

When they were fullest of wine and most flagrant in error,
Out of the sea rose a sign—out of Heaven a terror.
Then they saw, then they heard, then they knew—for none troubled
    to hide it,
An host had prepared their destruction, but still they denied it.

They denied what they dared not abide if it came to the trial;
But the Sword that was forged while they lied did not heed their denial.
It drove home, and no time was allowed to the crowd that was driven.
The preposterous-minded were cowed—they thought time would be
  given.
There was no need of a steed nor a lance to pursue them;
It was decreed their own deed, and not chance, should undo them.
The tares they had laughingly sown were ripe to the reaping.
The trust they had leagued to disown was removed from their keeping.
The eaters of other men's bread, the exempted from hardship,
The excusers of impotence fled, abdicating their wardship,
For the hate they had taught through the State brought the State
  no defender,
And it passed from the roll of the Nations in headlong surrender!

THE SONG OF SEVEN CITIES

I was Lord of Cities very sumptuously builded.
Seven roaring Cities paid me tribute from far.
Ivory their outposts were—the guardrooms of them gilded,
And garrisoned with Amazons invincible in war.

All the world went softly when it walked before my Cities—
Neither King nor Army vexed my peoples at their toil.
Never horse nor chariot irked or overbore my Cities.
Never Mob nor Ruler questioned whence they drew their spoil.

Banded, mailed and arrogant from sunrise unto sunset,
Singing while they sacked it, they possessed the land at large.
Yet when men would rob them, they resisted, they made onset
And pierced the smoke of battle with a thousand-sabred charge.

So they warred and trafficked only yesterday, my Cities.
Today there is no mark or mound of where my Cities stood.
For the River rose at midnight and it washed away my Cities.
They are evened with Atlantis and the towns before the Flood.

Rain on rain-gorged channels raised the water-levels round them,
Freshet backed on freshet swelled and swept their world from sight;
Till the emboldened floods linked arms and, flashing forward, drowned
    them—
Drowned my Seven Cities and their peoples in one night!

Low among the alders lie their derelict foundations,
The beams wherein they trusted and the plinths whereon they built—
My rulers and their treasure and their unborn populations,
Dead, destroyed, aborted, and defiled with mud and silt!

The Daughters of the Palace whom they cherished in my Cities,
My silver-tongued Princesses, and the promise of their May—
Their bridegrooms of the June-tide—all have perished in my Cities,
With the harsh envenomed virgins that can neither love nor play.

I was Lord of Cities—I will build anew my Cities,
Seven, set on rocks, above the wrath of any flood.
Nor will I rest from search till I have filled anew my Cities
With peoples undefeated of the dark, enduring blood.

To the sound of trumpets shall their seed restore my Cities,
Wealthy and well-weaponed, that once more may I behold
All the world go softly when it walks before my Cities,
And the horses and the chariots fleeing from them as of old!

THE BELL BUOY

They christened my brother of old—
And a saintly name he bears—
They gave him his place to hold
At the head of the belfry-stairs,
Where the minster-towers stand
And the breeding kestrels cry.
Would I change with my brother a league inland?
(Shoal! 'Ware[1] shoal!) Not I!

In the flush of the hot June prime,
O'er sleek flood-tides afire,
I hear him hurry the chime
To the bidding of checked Desire;
Till the sweated ringers tire
And the wild bob-majors[2] die.
Could I wait for my turn in the godly choir?
(Shoal! 'Ware shoal!) Not I!

When the smoking scud is blown—
When the greasy wind-rack lowers—
Apart and at peace and alone,
He counts the changeless hours.
He wars with darkling Powers
(I war with a darkling sea);
Would he stoop to my work in the gusty mirk?
(Shoal! 'Ware shoal!) Not he!

---

1. Beware.
2. A particular pattern of peals involving eight church bells.

16

There was never a priest to pray,
  There was never a hand to toll,
When they made me guard of the bay,
  And moored me over the shoal.
  I rock, I reel, and I roll—
My four great hammers ply—
  Could I speak or be still at the Church's will?
(Shoal! 'Ware shoal!) Not I!

The landward marks have failed,
  The fog-bank glides unguessed,
The seaward lights are veiled,
  The spent deep feigns her rest:
  But my ear is laid to her breast,
I lift to the swell—I cry!
  Could I wait in sloth on the Church's oath?
(Shoal! 'Ware shoal!) Not I!

At the careless end of night
  I thrill to the nearing screw;
I turn in the clearing light
  And I call to the drowsy crew;
  And the mud boils foul and blue
As the blind bow backs away.
  Will they give me their thanks if they clear the banks?
(Shoal! 'Ware shoal!) Not they!

The beach-pools cake and skim,
  The bursting spray-heads freeze,
I gather on crown and rim
  The grey, grained ice of the seas,
  Where, sheathed from bitt to trees,[3]
The plunging colliers[4] lie.
  Would I barter my place for the Church's grace?
(Shoal! 'Ware shoal!) Not I!

---

3. Posts on a ship's deck to which ropes and cables are fastened.
4. Coal ships.

Through the blur of the whirling snow,
    Or the black of the inky sleet,
The lanterns gather and grow,
    And I look for the homeward fleet.
    Rattle of block and sheet—
"Ready about—stand by!"
    Shall I ask them a fee ere they fetch the quay?
(Shoal! 'Ware shoal!) Not I!

I dip and I surge and I swing
    In the rip of the racing tide,
By the gates of doom I sing,
    On the horns of death I ride.
    A ship-length overside,
Between the course and the sand,
    Fretted and bound I bide
        Peril whereof I cry.
    Would I change with my brother a league inland?
(Shoal! 'Ware shoal!) Not I!

PROPHETS AT HOME

Prophets have honour all over the Earth,
  Except in the village where they were born,
Where such as knew them boys from birth
  Nature-ally hold 'em in scorn.

When Prophets are naughty and young and vain,
  They make a won'erful grievance of it;
(You can see by their writings how they complain),
  But O, 'tis won'erful good for the Prophet!

There's nothing Nineveh Town can give
  (Nor being swallowed by whales between),
Makes up for the place where a man's folk live,
  Which don't care nothing what he has been.
He might ha' been that, or he might ha' been this,
But they love and they hate him for what he is.

Part II

GOD AND MAN

A Song of the English (excerpt)

Fair is our lot—O goodly is our heritage!
(Humble ye, my people, and be fearful in your mirth!)
   For the Lord our God Most High
   He hath made the deep as dry,
He hath smote for us a pathway to the ends of all the Earth!

Yea, though we sinned—and our rulers went from righteousness—
Deep in all dishonour though we stained our garments' hem.
   Oh, be ye not dismayed,
   Though we stumbled and we strayed,
We were led by evil counsellors—the Lord shall deal with them!

Hold ye the Faith—the Faith our Fathers sealed us;
Whoring not with visions—overwise and overstale.
   Except ye pay the Lord
   Single heart and single sword,
Of your children in their bondage shall He ask them treble-tale!

Keep ye the Law—be swift in all obedience—
Clear the land of evil, drive the road and bridge the ford.
   Make ye sure to each his own
   That he reap where he hath sown;
By the peace among Our peoples let men know we serve the Lord!

What the People Said

By the well, where the bullocks go[1]
Silent and blind and slow—
By the field where the young corn dies
In the face of the sultry skies,
They have heard, as the dull Earth hears
The voice of the wind of an hour,
The sound of the Great Queen's voice:
"My God hath given me years,
Hath granted dominion and power:
And I bid you, O Land, rejoice."

And the ploughman settles the share
More deep in the grudging clod;
For he saith: "The wheat is my care,
And the rest is the will of God.
He sent the Mahratta spear[2]
As He sendeth the rain,
And the *Mlech,*[3] in the fated year,
Broke the spear in twain.
And was broken in turn. Who knows
How our Lords make strife?

---

1. This poem was written on the occasion of Queen Victoria's Golden Jubilee. "The People" referred to in the title are the peasants of India. Even though the fiftieth year of the queen's reign was celebrated around the world, it did nothing to benefit the poor people of India, who were under British rule. As the poem describes, the Indians had seen foreign rulers come and go—but the challenges and blessings of life simply went on.
2. The Mahratta were a tribe of warriors that ruled much of India from 1674 to 1818. They were replaced as a ruling power by the British East India Company.
3. Foreigner.

It is good that the young wheat grows,
For the bread is Life."

Then, far and near, as the twilight drew,
Hissed up to the scornful dark
Great serpents, blazing, of red and blue,
That rose and faded, and rose anew.
That the Land might wonder and mark
"Today is a day of days," they said,
"Make merry, O People, all!"
And the Ploughman listened and bowed his head:
"Today and tomorrow God's will," he said,
As he trimmed the lamps on the wall.

"He sendeth us years that are good,
As He sendeth the dearth,
He giveth to each man his food,
Or Her food to the Earth.
Our Kings and our Queens are afar—
On their peoples be peace—
God bringeth the rain to the Bar,
That our cattle increase."

And the Ploughman settled the share
More deep in the sun-dried clod:
"Mogul,[4] Mahratta, and *Mlech* from the North,
And White Queen over the Seas—
God raiseth them up and driveth them forth
As the dust of the ploughshare flies in the breeze;
But the wheat and the cattle are all my care,
And the rest is the will of God."

---

4. The Moguls, or Mughals, were invaders from central Asia who ruled large parts of India beginning in the sixteenth century.

"MY NEW-CUT ASHLAR"

My new-cut ashlar[1] takes the light
Where crimson-blank the windows flare.
By my own work before the night,
Great Overseer, I make my prayer.

If there be good in that I wrought
Thy Hand compelled it, Master, Thine—
Where I have failed to meet Thy Thought
I know, through Thee, the blame was mine.

One instant's toil to Thee denied
Stands all Eternity's offence.
Of that I did with Thee to guide,
To Thee, through Thee, be excellence.

The depth and dream of my desire,
The bitter paths wherein I stray—
Thou knowest Who hast made the Fire,
Thou knowest Who hast made the Clay.

Who, lest all thought of Eden fade,
Bring'st Eden to the craftsman's brain—
Godlike to muse o'er his own Trade
And manlike stand with God again!

---

1. In freemasonry, rough ashlar is rock in its natural state. Perfect ashlar has been cut, squared, and smoothed to fit exactly as needed in a building. In the same way, rough ashlar represents man in his natural state, while perfect ashlar symbolizes the master mason who is refined, has gained valuable knowledge, and lives an exemplary life. Kipling was an adherent of freemasonry through most of his adult life.

One stone the more swings to her place[2]
   In that dread Temple of Thy worth.
It is enough that, thro' Thy Grace,
   I saw nought common on Thy Earth.

Take not that vision from my ken—
   Oh, whatsoe'er may spoil or speed.
Help me to need no aid from men
   That I may help such men as need!

---

2. As early as medieval times, stonemasons used cranes to move heavy stones into place.

DEDICATION FROM "BARRACK-ROOM BALLADS"

Beyond the path of the outmost sun through utter darkness hurled—
Farther than ever comet flared or vagrant star-dust swirled—
Live such as fought and sailed and ruled and loved and made our world.

They are purged of pride because they died; they know the worth
    of their bays;[1]
They sit at wine with the Maidens Nine[2] and the Gods of the Elder
    Days—
It is their will to serve or be still as fitteth Our Father's praise.

'Tis theirs to sweep through the ringing deep where Azrael's outposts
    are,[3]
Or buffet a path through the Pit's[4] red wrath when God goes out to war,
Or hang with the reckless Seraphim[5] on the rein of a red-maned star.

They take their mirth in the joy of the Earth—they dare not grieve
    for her pain;
They know of toil and the end of toil; they know God's Law is plain;
So they whistle the Devil to make them sport who know that Sin is vain.

And oft-times cometh our wise Lord God, master of every trade,
And tells them tales of His daily toil, of Edens newly made;
And they rise to their feet as He passes by, gentlemen unafraid.

---

1. Bays represent an honorary garland or crown given for victory or excellence.

2. This may represent the Valkyrie in Norse mythology, female figures with power to choose those who would die in battle and who would live; they often were seen in groups of nine. Those who were slain were allowed to go to Valhalla, where they drank mead with the Valkyries.

3. Azrael is the angel of death in Hebrew lore, Islam, and Sikhism.

4. A word for hell in the Bible. See, for example, Psalm 30:3, 9; Isaiah 14:15; Revelation 9:1-2.

5. Celestial or heavenly beings in Jewish and Christian belief. See Isaiah 6:1-8;

To these who are cleansed of base Desire, Sorrow and Lust and Shame—
Gods for they knew the hearts of men, men for they stooped to Fame—
Borne on the breath that men call Death, my brother's spirit came.[6]

He scarce had need to doff his pride or slough the dross of Earth—
E'en as he trod that day to God so walked he from his birth,
In simpleness and gentleness and honour and clean mirth.

So cup to lip in fellowship they gave him welcome high
And made him place at the banquet board—the Strong Men ranged
  thereby,
Who had done his work and held his peace and had no fear to die.

Beyond the loom of the last lone star, through open darkness hurled,
Further than rebel comet dared or hiving star-swarm swirled,
Sits he with those that praise our God for that they served His world.

---

6. Wolcott Balestier, a close friend and sometime collaborator with Kipling, died of typhoid fever in 1891. He would have been Kipling's brother-in-law; Kipling married Wolcott's sister Caroline a few weeks after Wolcott's death. In some editions, this poem was dedicated to Wolcott Balestier.

NEW LAMPS FOR OLD

When the flush of the newborn sun fell first on Eden's green and gold,
A Lying Spirit sat under the Tree and sang, "New Lamps for Old!"[1]
And Adam waked from his mighty sleep, and Eve was at his side,
And the twain had faith in the song that they heard, and knew not
    the Spirit lied.[2]

They plucked a lamp from the Eden-tree (the ancient legend saith),
And lighted themselves the Path of Toil that runs to the Gate of Death;
They left the lamp for the joy of their sons, and that was a glorious gain,
When the Spirit cried, "New Lamps for Old!" in the ear of the branded
    Cain.[3]

So he gat fresh hope, and builded a town, and watched his breed
    increase,
Till Tubal[4] lighted the Lamp of War from the flickering Lamp of Peace;
And ever they fought with fire and sword and travailed in hate and fear,
As the Spirit sang, "New Lamps for Old!" at the change of the changing
    year.

They sought new lamps in the Morning-red, they sought new lamps
    in the West,
Till the waters covered the pitiful land and the heart of the world
    had rest

---

1. In the Arabian folk tale about Aladdin's magic lamp, Aladdin was tricked into
trading his priceless (but unattractive) old lamp for a worthless (but shiny) new one.
2. See Genesis 2-3.
3. See Genesis 4:15.
4. See Genesis 4:22.

Had rest with the Rain of the Forty Days, but the Ark rode safe above,
And the Spirit cried, "New Lamps for Old!" when Noah loosened the
    Dove.[5]

And some say now that the Eden-tree had never a root on earth;
And some say now from an eyeless eft[6] our Father Adam had birth;
And some say now there was never an Ark and never a God to save;
And some say now that Man is a God, and some say Man is a slave;

And some build altars East and West, and some build North and South;
And some bow down to the Work of the Hand and some to the Word
    of the Mouth.
But wheresoever a heart may beat or a hand reach forth to hold,
The Spirit comes with the coming year, and cries, "New Lamps for Old!"

And the sons of Adam leave their toil who are cursed with the Curse
    of Hope,
And hang the profitless past in a noose of the thundering belfry's rope,
And tear the branch from the laurel-bush with feastings manifold,
When the cry goes up to the scornful stars, "New Lamps! New Lamps
    for Old!"

Though all the lamps that ever were lit have winked at the world
    for years,
The sons of Adam crowd the streets with laughter and sighs and tears;
For they hold that new, strange lamps shall shine to guide their feet
    aright,
And they turn their eyes to the scornful stars and stretch their arms
    to the night.

And the Spirit gives them the Lamp of War that burns at the cannon-lip,
As it blazed on the point of Tubal's blade and the prow of the battleship;
And the Lamp of Love that was Eve's to snatch from Lilith[7] under
    the Tree;
And the Lamp of Fame that is old as Strife and dim as Memory;

---

5. See Genesis 6-8.
6. The juvenile stage of a newt, an amphibian creature.
7. An early rabbinical tradition claims that Lilith was Adam's first wife. After she
rebelled and abandoned Adam, according to this tradition, God created Eve.

And the Lamp of Faith that was won from Job, and of Shame that
    was wrung from Cain;
And the Lamp of Youth that was Adam's once, and the cold blue Lamp
    of Pain;
And last is the terrible Lamp of Hope that every man must bear,
Lest he find his peace ere the day of his death by the light of the
    Lamp Despair.

We know that the Eden Lamp is lost,—if ever were Eden made,
And the ink of the Schools[8] in the Lamp of Faith has sunk a world
    in the shade;
But ever we look for a light that is new, and ever the Spirit cries,
"New Lamps for Old!" and we take the lamps, and—behold, the Spirit
    lies!

---

8. Scholars in the medieval era.

THE EXPLORER

"There's no sense in going further—it's the edge of cultivation,"
  So they said, and I believed it—broke my land and sowed my crop—
Built my barns and strung my fences in the little border station
  Tucked away below the foothills where the trails run out and stop:

Till a voice, as bad as Conscience, rang interminable changes
  On one everlasting Whisper day and night repeated—so:
"Something hidden. Go and find it. Go and look behind the Ranges—
  Something lost behind the Ranges. Lost and waiting for you. Go!"

So I went, worn out of patience; never told my nearest neighbours—
  Stole away with pack and ponies—left 'em drinking in the town;
And the faith that moveth mountains[1] didn't seem to help my labours
  As I faced the sheer main-ranges, whipping up and leading down.

March by march I puzzled through 'em, turning flanks and dodging
    shoulders,
  Hurried on in hope of water, headed back for lack of grass;
Till I camped above the tree-line—drifted snow and naked boulders—
  Felt free air astir to windward—knew I'd stumbled on the Pass.

'Thought to name it for the finder: but that night the Norther found
    me—
  Froze and killed the plains-bred ponies; so I called the camp Despair
(It's the Railway Gap today, though). Then my Whisper waked to
    hound me:—
  "Something lost behind the Ranges. Over yonder! Go you there!"

---

1. Matthew 21:21.

Then I knew, the while I doubted—knew His Hand was certain o'er me.
  Still—it might be self-delusion—scores of better men had died—
I could reach the township living, but . . . He knows what terror tore
      me . . .
  But I didn't . . . but I didn't. I went down the other side.

Till the snow ran out in flowers, and the flowers turned to aloes,
  And the aloes sprung to thickets and a brimming stream ran by;
But the thickets dwined[2] to thorn-scrub, and the water drained to
      shallows,
  And I dropped again on desert—blasted earth, and blasting sky. . . .

I remember lighting fires; I remember sitting by 'em;
  I remember seeing faces, hearing voices, through the smoke;
I remember they were fancy[3]—for I threw a stone to try 'em.
  "Something lost behind the Ranges" was the only word they spoke.

I remember going crazy. I remember that I knew it
  When I heard myself hallooing to the funny folk I saw.
Very full of dreams that desert, but my two legs took me through it . . .
  And I used to watch 'em moving with the toes all black and raw.

But at last the country altered—White Man's country past disputing[4]—
  Rolling grass and open timber, with a hint of hills behind—
There I found me food and water, and I lay a week recruiting.[5]
  Got my strength and lost my nightmares. Then I entered on my find.

Thence I ran my first rough survey—chose my trees and blazed and
      ringed 'em—
  Week by week I pried and sampled—week by week my findings grew.
Saul he went to look for donkeys, and by God he found a kingdom![6]
  But by God, who sent His Whisper, I had struck the worth of two!

Up along the hostile mountains, where the hair-poised snowslide
      shivers—
  Down and through the big fat marshes that the virgin ore-bed stains,
Till I heard the mile-wide mutterings of unimagined rivers,
  And beyond the nameless timber saw illimitable plains!

---

2. Dwindled.
3. Imagined.
4. Country with a temperate climate.
5. Recuperating.
6. 1 Samuel 9:3-27; 10:1-24.

'Plotted sites of future cities, traced the easy grades between 'em;
  Watched unharnessed rapids wasting fifty thousand head[7] an hour;
Counted leagues of water-frontage through the axe-ripe woods that
    screen 'em—
Saw the plant to feed a people—up and waiting for the power!

Well I know who'll take the credit—all the clever chaps that followed—
  Came, a dozen men together—never knew my desert-fears;
Tracked me by the camps I'd quitted, used the water-holes I hollowed.
  They'll go back and do the talking. *They'll* be called the Pioneers!

They will find my sites of townships—not the cities that I set there.
  They will rediscover rivers—not my rivers heard at night.
By my own old marks and bearings they will show me how to get there,
  By the lonely cairns I builded they will guide my feet aright.

Have I named one single river? Have I claimed one single acre?
  Have I kept one single nugget—(barring samples)? No, not I!
Because my price was paid me ten times over by my Maker.
  But you wouldn't understand it. You go up and occupy.

Ores you'll find there; wood and cattle; water-transit sure and steady
  (That should keep the railway rates down), coal and iron at your
    doors.
God took care to hide that country till He judged His people ready,
  Then He chose me for His Whisper, and I've found it, and it's yours!

Yes, your "Never-never country"—yes, your "edge of cultivation"
  And "no sense in going further"—till I crossed the range to see.
God forgive me! No, *I* didn't. It's God's present to our nation.
  Anybody might have found it, but—His Whisper came to Me!

---

7. A unit of water power.

THE RABBI'S SONG

2 Samuel 14:14[1]

If Thought can reach to Heaven,
    On Heaven let it dwell,
For fear the Thought be given
    Like power to reach to Hell.
For fear the desolation
    And darkness of thy mind
Perplex an habitation
    Which thou hast left behind.

Let nothing linger after—
    No whimpering ghost remain,
In wall, or beam, or rafter,
    Of any hate or pain.
Cleanse and call home thy spirit,
    Deny her leave to cast,
On aught thy heirs inherit,
    The shadow of her past.

For think, in all thy sadness,
    What road our griefs may take;
Whose brain reflect our madness,
    Or whom our terrors shake:

---

1. "For we must needs die, and are as water spilt on the ground, which cannot be gathered up again; neither doth God respect any person: yet doth he devise means, that his banished be not expelled from him."

For think, lest any languish
   By cause of thy distress—
The arrows of our anguish
   Fly farther than we guess.

Our lives, our tears, as water,
   Are spilled upon the ground;
God giveth no man quarter,
   Yet God a means hath found,
Though faith and hope have vanished,
   And even love grows dim—
A means whereby His banished
   Be not expelled from Him!

A Carol

Our Lord Who did the Ox command[1]
   To kneel to Judah's King,
He binds His frost upon the land
   To ripen it for Spring—
To ripen it for Spring, good sirs,
   According to His Word.
Which well must be as ye can see—
And who shall judge the Lord?

When we poor fenmen[2] skate the ice
   Or shiver on the wold,[3]
We hear the cry of a single tree[4]
   That breaks her heart in the cold—
That breaks her heart in the cold, good sirs,
   And rendeth by the board;
Which well must be as ye can see—
And who shall judge the Lord?

Her wood is crazed[5] and little worth
   Excepting as to burn,
That we may warm and make our mirth
   Until the Spring return—

---

1. This poem is written to the same meter and with the same pattern as medieval carol, "Joys Seven," which begins, "The first good joy that Mary had . . ."
2. The marshes in eastern England, called "the fens," are often flooded and frozen in cold, wet winters.
3. Countryside.
4. A reference to the cross on which Christ was crucified.
5. Cracked.

Until the Spring return, good sirs,
   When Christians walk abroad;
When well must be as ye can see—
   And who shall judge the Lord?

God bless the master of this house,
   And all who sleep therein!
And guard the fens from pirate folk,
   And keep us all from sin,
To walk in honesty, good sirs,
   Of thought and deed and word!
Which shall befriend our latter end. . . .
   And who shall judge the Lord?

COLD IRON

Gold is for the mistress—silver for the maid—
Copper for the craftsman cunning at his trade."
"Good!" said the Baron, sitting in his hall,
"But Iron—Cold Iron—is master of them all."

So he made rebellion 'gainst the King his liege,
Camped before his citadel and summoned it to siege.
"Nay!" said the cannoneer on the castle wall,
"But Iron—Cold Iron—shall be master of you all!"

Woe for the Baron and his knights so strong,
When the cruel cannon-balls laid 'em all along;
He was taken prisoner, he was cast in thrall,
And Iron—Cold Iron—was master of it all!

Yet his King spake kindly (ah, how kind a Lord!)
"What if I release thee now and give thee back thy sword?"
"Nay!" said the Baron, "mock not at my fall,
For Iron—Cold Iron—is master of men all."

"Tears are for the craven, prayers are for the clown—
Halters for the silly neck that cannot keep a crown."
"As my loss is grievous, so my hope is small,
For Iron—Cold Iron—must be master of men all!"

Yet his King made answer (few such Kings there be!)
"Here is Bread and here is Wine—sit and sup with me.
Eat and drink in Mary's Name, the whiles I do recall
How Iron—Cold Iron—can be master of men all!"

He took the Wine and blessed it. He blessed and brake the Bread.
With His own Hands He served Them, and presently He said:
"See! These Hands they pierced with nails, outside My city wall,
Show Iron—Cold Iron—to be master of men all."

"Wounds are for the desperate, blows are for the strong.
Balm and oil for weary hearts all cut and bruised with wrong.
I forgive thy treason—I redeem thy fall—
For Iron—Cold Iron—must be master of men all!"

"Crowns are for the valiant—sceptres for the bold!
Thrones and powers for mighty men who dare to take and hold!"
"Nay!" said the Baron, kneeling in his hall,
"But Iron—Cold Iron—is master of men all!
Iron out of Calvary is master of men all!"

THE SACK OF THE GODS

Strangers drawn from the ends of the earth, jewelled and plumed
  were we;
I was Lord of the Inca race, and she was Queen of the Sea.
Under the stars beyond our stars where the new-forged meteors glow,
Hotly we stormed Valhalla,[1] a million years ago!

Ever 'neath high Valhalla Hall the well-tuned horns begin,
When the swords are out in the underworld, and the weary Gods come in.
Ever through high Valhalla Gate the Patient Angel goes.
He opens the eyes that are blind with hate—he joins the hands of foes.

Dust of the stars was under our feet, glitter of stars above—
Wrecks of our wrath dropped reeling down as we fought and we
  spurned and we strove.
Worlds upon worlds we tossed aside, and scattered them to and fro,
The night that we stormed Valhalla, a million years ago!

They are forgiven as they forgive all those dark wounds and deep,
Their beds are made on the Lap of Time and they lie down and sleep.
They are forgiven as they forgive all those old wounds that bleed.
They shut their eyes from their worshippers; they sleep till the world
  has need.

She with the star I had marked for my own—I with my set desire—
Lost in the loom of the Night of Nights—lighted by worlds afire—
Met in a war against the Gods where the headlong meteors glow,
Hewing our way to Valhalla, a million years ago!

They will come back—come back again, as long as the red Earth rolls.
He never wasted a leaf or a tree. Do you think He would squander souls?

---

1. In Norse mythology, Valhalla is the great hall in Asgard where slain heroes go. The ruler of Valhalla was Odin, viewed by many to be the father of all the gods.

42

THE HOLY WAR

"For here lay the excellent wisdom of him that built Mansoul, that the walls could never be broken down nor hurt by the most mighty adverse potentate unless the townsmen gave consent thereto."

—*John Bunyan's* Holy War

A tinker out of Bedford,
  A vagrant oft in quod,[1]
A private under Fairfax,[2]
  A minister of God—
Two hundred years and thirty
  Ere Armageddon came
His single hand portrayed it,
  And Bunyan was his name!

He mapped for those who follow,
  The world in which we are—
"This famous town of Mansoul"
  That takes the Holy War.[3]
Her true and traitor people,
  The Gates along her wall,
From Eye Gate unto Feel Gate,[4]
  John Bunyan showed them all.

---

1. An archaic term for jail.
2. Bunyan served under Lord Fairfax in the English Civil War.
3. In 1682, Bunyan published the book *The Holy War Made by King Shaddai Upon Diabolus, to Regain the Metropolis of the World, Or, The Losing and Taking Again of the Town of Mansoul.* In the novel, the town of Mansoul forsakes their king for Diabolus. The novel is an allegory of the battle between God and the devil for the soul of man.
4. One could enter Mansoul by five gates, each named after one of the five senses.

All enemy divisions,
   Recruits of every class,
And highly-screened positions
   For flame or poison-gas;
The craft that we call modern,
   The crimes that we call new,
John Bunyan had 'em typed and filed
   In Sixteen Eighty-two.

Likewise the Lords of Looseness
   That hamper faith and works,
The Perseverance-Doubters,
   And Present-Comfort shirks,
With brittle intellectuals
   Who crack beneath a strain—
John Bunyan met that helpful set
   In Charles the Second's reign.

Emmanuel's[5] vanguard dying
   For right and not for rights,
My Lord Apollyon[6] lying
   To the State-kept Stockholmites,
The Pope, the swithering Neutrals
   The Kaiser and his Gott—
Their roles, their goals, their naked souls—
   He knew and drew the lot.

Now he hath left his quarters,
   In Bunhill Fields to lie,
The wisdom that he taught us
   Is proven prophecy—
One watchword through our Armies,
   One answer from our Lands:—
"No dealings with Diabolus
   As long as Mansoul stands!"

---

5. The son of Shaddai, the founder of Mansoul. El Shaddai is a Hebrew name of God.
6. One of the primary helpers of Diabolus.

A pedlar from a hovel,
   The lowest of the low—
The Father of the Novel,
   Salvation's first Defoe,
Eight blinded generations
   Ere Armageddon came,
He showed us how to meet it,
   And Bunyan was his name!

ZION

The Doorkeepers of Zion,[1]
  They do not always stand
In helmet and whole armour,
  With halberds in their hand;
But, being sure of Zion,
  And all her mysteries,
They rest awhile in Zion,
Sit down and smile in Zion;
Ay, even jest in Zion;
  In Zion, at their ease.

The Gatekeepers of Baal,[2]
  They dare not sit or lean,
But fume and fret and posture
  And foam and curse between;
For being bound to Baal,
  Whose sacrifice is vain,
Their rest is scant with Baal,
They glare and pant for Baal,
They mouth and rant for Baal,
  For Baal in their pain!

---

1. Zion is the name of a mountain in Jerusalem, on which the Jewish temple was built. It symbolizes all the hopes and desires of the Jewish people.
2. Baal was a false God often mentioned in the Old Testament.

But we will go to Zion,
   By choice and not through dread,
With these our present comrades
   And those our present dead;[3]
And, being free of Zion
   In both her fellowships,[4]
Sit down and sup in Zion—
Stand up and drink in Zion
Whatever cup[5] in Zion
   Is offered to our lips!

3. Those who had recently died. Surely this would include Kipling's own son, John, who was killed during World War I in the Battle of Loos in 1915.
4. The fellowship of the living as well as the dead.
5. The cup can be a cup of blessing or of bitterness (see Psalm 23:5; Matthew 26:39).

THE CHILDREN'S SONG (EXCERPT)

Father in Heaven who lovest all,
Oh, help Thy children when they call;
That they may build from age to age
An undefiled heritage.

Teach us to bear the yoke in youth,[1]
With steadfastness and careful truth;
That, in our time, Thy Grace may give
The Truth whereby the Nations live.

Teach us to rule ourselves alway,
Controlled and cleanly night and day;
That we may bring, if need arise,
No maimed or worthless sacrifice.[2]

Teach us to look in all our ends
On Thee for judge, and not our friends;
That we, with Thee, may walk uncowed
By fear or favour of the crowd.

Teach us the Strength that cannot seek,
By deed or thought, to hurt the weak;
That, under Thee, we may possess
Man's strength to comfort man's distress.

Teach us Delight in simple things,
And Mirth that has no bitter springs;
Forgiveness free of evil done,
And Love to all men 'neath the sun!

---

1. See Lamentations 3:27.
2. See Leviticus 22:18-22; Malachi 1:13-14.

THE ANSWER

A Rose, in tatters on the garden path,
Cried out to God and murmured 'gainst His Wrath,
Because a sudden wind at twilight's hush
Had snapped her stem alone of all the bush.
And God, Who hears both sun-dried dust and sun,
Had pity, whispering to that luckless one,
"Sister, in that thou sayest We did not well—
What voices heardst thou when thy petals fell?"
And the Rose answered, "In that evil hour
A voice said, 'Father, wherefore falls the flower?
For lo, the very gossamers are still.'
And a voice answered, 'Son, by Allah's will!'"

Then softly as a rain-mist on the sward,
Came to the Rose the Answer of the Lord:
"Sister, before We smote the Dark in twain,
Ere yet the stars saw one another plain,
Time, Tide, and Space, We bound unto the task
That thou shouldst fall, and such an one should ask."
Whereat the withered flower, all content,
Died as they die whose days are innocent;
While he who questioned why the flower fell
Caught hold of God and saved his soul from Hell.

REBIRTH

If any God should say,
"I will restore
The world her yesterday
Whole as before
My Judgment blasted it"—who would not lift
Heart, eye, and hand in passion o'er the gift?

If any God should will
To wipe from mind
The memory of this ill
Which is mankind
In soul and substance now—who would not bless
Even to tears His loving-tenderness?

If any God should give
Us leave to fly
These present deaths we live,
And safely die
In those lost lives we lived ere we were born—
What man but would not laugh the excuse to scorn?

For we are what we are—
So broke[1] to blood
And the strict works of war—
So long subdued
To sacrifice, that threadbare Death commands
Hardly observance at our busier hands.

---

1. This uses "broke" with the same meaning as is used in breaking horses. When we are "broke" in this sense, we become submissive and accustomed to the demands of our master.

Yet we were what we were,
And, fashioned so,
It pleases us to stare
At the far show
Of unbelievable years and shapes that flit,
In our own likeness, on the edge of it.

THE CHOICE

The American Spirit Speaks:

To the Judge of Right and Wrong
  With Whom fulfillment lies
Our purpose and our power belong,
  Our faith and sacrifice.

Let Freedom's Land[1] rejoice!
  Our ancient bonds are riven;
Once more to us the eternal choice
  Of Good or Ill is given.

Not at a little cost,
  Hardly by prayer or tears,
Shall we recover the road we lost
  In the drugged and doubting years,[2]

But, after the fires and the wrath,
  But, after searching and pain,
His Mercy opens us a path
  To live with ourselves again.

In the Gates of Death rejoice!
  We see and hold the good—
Bear witness, Earth, we have made our choice[3]
  With Freedom's brotherhood![4]

---

1. The United States of America.
2. The years in which the United States was neutral during World War I.
3. The United States entered the war against Germany on April 6, 1917.
4. The nations that were allied against Germany.

Then praise the Lord Most High
Whose Strength hath saved us whole,
Who bade us choose that the Flesh should die
And not the living Soul!

To the God in man displayed—
Where'er we see that Birth,
Be love and understanding paid
As never yet on earth!

To the Spirit that moves in Man,
On Whom all worlds depend,
Be Glory since our world began
And service to the end!

A PILGRIM'S WAY

I do not look for holy saints to guide me on my way,
Or male and female devilkins to lead my feet astray.
If these are added, I rejoice—if not, I shall not mind,
So long as I have leave and choice to meet my fellow-kind.
   For as we come and as we go (and deadly-soon go we!)
   The people, Lord, Thy people, are good enough for me!

Thus I will honour pious men whose virtue shines so bright
(Though none are more amazed than I when I by chance do right),
And I will pity foolish men for woe their sins have bred
(Though ninety-nine percent of mine I brought on my own head).
   And, Amorite or Eremite,[1] or General Averagee,
   The people, Lord, Thy people, are good enough for me!

And when they bore me overmuch, I will not shake mine ears,
Recalling many thousand such whom I have bored to tears.
And when they labour to impress, I will not doubt nor scoff;
Since I myself have done no less and—sometimes pulled it off.
   Yea, as we are and we are not, and we pretend to be,
   The people, Lord, Thy people, are good enough for me!

And when they work me random wrong, as oftentimes hath been,
I will not cherish hate too long (my hands are none too clean).
And when they do me random good I will not feign surprise;
No more than those whom I have cheered with wayside charities.
   But, as we give and as we take—whate'er our takings be—
   The people, Lord, Thy people, are good enough for me!

---

1. Amorites were an ancient Semitic people in southern Mesopotamia. In the Bible they inhabited the land of Canaan and were described as giants (see Amos 2:9). An eremite was a Christian hermit or recluse.

But when I meet with frantic folk who sinfully declare
There is no pardon for their sin, the same I will not spare
Till I have proved that Heaven and Hell which in our hearts we have
Show nothing irredeemable on either side the grave.
    For as we live and as we die—if utter Death there be—
    The people, Lord, Thy people, are good enough for me!

Deliver me from every pride—the Middle, High, and Low—
That bars me from a brother's side, whatever pride he show.
And purge me from all heresies of thought and speech and pen
That bid me judge him otherwise than I am judged. *Amen!*
    That I may sing of Crowd or King or road-borne company,
    That I may labour in my day, vocation and degree,

To prove the same in deed and name, and hold unshakenly
(Where'er I go, whate'er I know, whoe'er my neighbour be)
This single faith in Life and Death and all Eternity:
"The people, Lord, Thy people, are good enough for me!"

THE SUPPORTS

(Song of the Waiting Seraphs)[1]

FULL CHORUS
To Him Who bade the Heavens abide, yet cease not from their motion,
To Him Who tames the moonstruck tide a day round the Ocean—
Let His Names be magnified in all poor folks' devotion!

POWERS AND GIFTS
Not for Prophecies or Powers, Visions, Gifts, or Graces,
But the unregardful hours that grind us in our places
With the burden on our backs, the weather in our faces.

TOILS
Not for any Miracle of easy Loaves and Fishes,
But for doing, 'gainst our will, work against our wishes—
Such as finding food to fill daily-emptied dishes.

GLORIES
Not for Voices, Harps or Wings or rapt illumination,
But the grosser Self that springs of use and occupation,
Unto which the Spirit clings as her last salvation.

POWERS, GLORIES, TOILS, AND GIFTS
(He Who launched our Ship of Fools many anchors gave us,
Lest one gale should start them all—one collision stave us.
  Praise Him for the petty creeds
  That prescribe in paltry needs
Solemn rites to trivial deeds and, by small things, save us!)

---

1. This seems to be a song sung from paradise. The seraphs (a form of angels) are named at the head of each section: Powers and Gifts, Toils, Glories, and so forth.

56

SERVICES AND LOVES
Heart may fail, and Strength outwear, and Purpose turn to Loathing,
But the everyday affair of business, meals, and clothing,
Builds the bulkhead 'twixt Despair and the Edge of Nothing.

PATIENCES
(Praise Him, then, Who orders it that, though Earth be flaring,
 And the crazy skies are lit
  By the searchlights of the Pit,
Man should not depart a whit from his wonted bearing.)

HOPES
He Who bids the wild-swans' host still maintain their flight on
 Air-roads over islands lost—
 Ages since 'neath Ocean lost—
Beaches of some sunken coast their fathers would alight on—

FAITHS
He shall guide us through this dark, not by new-blown glories,
But by every ancient mark our fathers used before us,
Till our children ground their ark where the proper shore is.

SERVICES, PATIENCES, FAITHS, HOPES, AND LOVES
He Who used the clay that clings on our boots to make us,
Shall not suffer earthly things to remove or shake us:
 But, when Man denies His Lord,
 Habit without Fleet or Sword
 (Custom without threat or word)
Sees the ancient fanes[2] restored—the timeless rites o'ertake us!

FULL CHORUS
For He Who makes the Mountains smoke and rives the Hill asunder,
 And, tomorrow, leads the grass—
 Mere unconquerable grass—
Where the fuming crater was, to heal and hide it under,
 He shall not—He shall not—
Shall not lay on us the yoke of too long Fear and Wonder!

---

2. Temples or shrines.

RECESSIONAL

God of our fathers, known of old—
  Lord of our far-flung battle line—
Beneath whose awful hand we hold
  Dominion over palm and pine—
Lord God of Hosts, be with us yet,
Lest we forget—lest we forget!

The tumult and the shouting dies—
  The Captains and the Kings depart—
Still stands Thine ancient sacrifice,
  An humble and a contrite heart.
Lord God of Hosts, be with us yet,
Lest we forget—lest we forget!

Far-called our navies melt away—
  On dune and headland sinks the fire—
Lo, all our pomp of yesterday
  Is one with Nineveh and Tyre!
Judge of the Nations, spare us yet,
Lest we forget—lest we forget!

If, drunk with sight of power, we loose
  Wild tongues that have not Thee in awe—
Such boastings as the Gentiles use,
  Or lesser breeds without the Law—
Lord God of Hosts, be with us yet,
Lest we forget—lest we forget!

For heathen heart that puts her trust
   In reeking tube and iron shard—
All valiant dust that builds on dust,
   And guarding calls not Thee to guard.
For frantic boast and foolish word,
Thy Mercy on Thy People, Lord!
                    Amen.

THE PRAYER OF MIRIAM COHEN

From the wheel and the drift of Things
Deliver us, Good Lord,
And we will face the wrath of Kings,
The faggot and the sword!

Lay not thy Works before our eyes
Nor vex us with thy Wars,
Lest we should feel the straining skies
O'ertrod by trampling stars.

Hold us secure behind the gates
Of saving flesh and bone,
Lest we should dream what Dream awaits
The Soul escaped alone.

Thy Path, thy Purposes conceal
From our beleaguered realm
Lest any shattering whisper steal
Upon us and o'erwhelm.

A veil 'twixt us and Thee, Good Lord,
A veil 'twixt us and Thee—
Lest we should hear too clear, too clear,
And unto madness see!

Part III

LIFE AND DEATH

"By the Hoof of the Wild Goat"

By the Hoof of the Wild Goat uptossed
From the cliff where she lay in the Sun
  Fell the Stone
To the Tarn[1] where the daylight is lost,
So she fell from the light of the Sun
  And alone!

Now the fall was ordained from the first
With the Goat and the Cliff and the Tarn,
  But the Stone
Knows only her life is accursed
As she sinks from the light of the Sun
  And alone!

Oh Thou Who hast builded the World,
Oh Thou Who hast lighted the Sun,
Oh Thou Who hast darkened the Tarn,
  Judge Thou
The sin of the Stone that was hurled
By the goat from the light of the Sun,
As she sinks in the mire of the Tarn,
  Even now—even now—even now!

---

1. A type of small lake in northern England.

EVIL LAND

We meet in an evil land
  That is near to the gates of hell.
I wait for thy command
To serve, to speed or withstand.
  And thou sayest, I do not well?

Oh Love, the flowers so red
  Be only blossoms of flame,
The earth is full of the dead,
The new-killed, restless dead.
There is danger beneath and o'erhead.
  And I guard thy gates in fear
    Of peril and jeopardy,
  Of words thou canst not hear,
    Of signs thou canst not see—
  And thou sayest 'tis ill that I came?

An Old Song

So long as 'neath the Kalka hills[1]
  The tonga-horn[2] shall ring,
So long as down the Solon dip
  The hard-held ponies swing,
So long as Tara Devi[3] sees
  The lights of Simla town,
So long as Pleasure calls us up,
  Or Duty drives us down,
    If you love me as I love you
    What pair so happy as we two?

So long as Aces take the King,
  Or backers take the bet,
So long as debt leads men to wed,
  Or marriage leads to debt,
So long as little luncheons, Love,
  And scandal hold their vogue,
While there is sport at Annandale
  Or whisky at Jutogh,
    If you love me as I love you
    What knife can cut our love in two?

---

1. Kalka and Simla are villages at the foot of the Himalayas. Solon is a railway station between the two. Other locations mentioned in the poem are nearby.
2. A horn attached to a cart drawn by horses.
3. A temple goddess.

So long as down the rocking floor
  The raving polka spins,
So long as Kitchen Lancers[4] spur
  The maddened violins,
So long as through the whirling smoke
  We hear the oft-told tale—
"Twelve hundred in the Lotteries,"
  And What's-her-name for sale,
    If you love me as I love you
    We'll play the game and win it too.

So long as Lust or Lucre tempt
  Straight riders from the course,
So long as with each drink we pour
  Black brewage of Remorse,
So long as those unloaded guns[5]
  We keep beside the bed,
Blow off, by obvious accident,
  The lucky owner's head,
    If you love me as I love you
    What can Life kill or Death undo?

So long as Death 'twixt dance and dance
  Chills best and bravest blood,
And drops the reckless rider down
  The rotten, rain-soaked *khud*,[6]
So long as rumours from the North
  Make loving wives afraid,
So long as Burma takes the boy
  Or typhoid kills the maid,
    If you love me as I love you
    What knife can cut our love in two?

By all that lights our daily life
  Or works our lifelong woe,
From Boileaugunge to Simla Downs
  And those grim glades below,
Where, heedless of the flying hoof

---

4. A lively dance for ladies and gentlemen.
5. Ironic—the guns are not really unloaded.
6. A steep hillside or deep valley.

And clamour overhead,
Sleep, with the grey-langur[7] for guard
Our very scornful Dead,
    If you love me as I love you
    All Earth is servant to us two!

By Docket, Billetdoux, and File,[8]
By Mountain, Cliff, and Fir,
By Fan and Sword and Office-box,[9]
By Corset, Plume,[10] and Spur
By Riot, Revel, Waltz, and War,
  By Women, Work, and Bills,
By all the life that fizzes in
The everlasting Hills,
    If you love me as I love you
    What pair so happy as we two?

---

7. A great ape that lives in the area; Hindus saw it as divine.
8. Forms of paperwork. A *billetdoux* is a love letter.
9. Probably a portable desk.
10. The tuft a soldier would wear on his head-dress.

THE SONG OF THE DEAD

Hear now the Song of the Dead—in the North by the torn berg-edges—
They that look still to the Pole, asleep by their hide-stripped sledges.
Song of the Dead in the South—in the sun by their skeleton horses,
Where the warrigal[1] whimpers and bays through the dust of the sere
river-courses.

Song of the Dead in the East—in the heat-rotted jungle-hollows,
Where the dog-ape barks in the kloof[2]—in the brake of the buffalo-
wallows.

Song of the Dead in the West in the Barrens, the pass that betrayed them,
Where the wolverine tumbles their packs from the camp and the grave-
mound they made them;
        Hear now the Song of the Dead!

I

We were dreamers, dreaming greatly, in the man-stifled town;
We yearned beyond the sky-line where the strange roads go down.
Came the Whisper, came the Vision, came the Power with the Need,
Till the Soul that is not man's soul was lent us to lead.
As the deer breaks—as the steer breaks—from the herd where they
    graze,
In the faith of little children we went on our ways.
Then the wood failed—then the food failed—then the last water dried.
In the faith of little children we lay down and died.
On the sand-drift—on the veldt-side—in the fern-scrub we lay,

---

1. Australian wild dog, also known as a dingo.
2. Gorge or mountain pass.

That our sons might follow after by the bones on the way.
Follow after—follow after! We have watered the root,
And the bud has come to blossom that ripens for fruit!
Follow after—we are waiting, by the trails that we lost,
For the sounds of many footsteps, for the tread of a host.
Follow after—follow after—for the harvest is sown:
By the bones about the wayside ye shall come to your own! . . .

II

We have fed our sea for a thousand years
 And she calls us, still unfed,
Though there's never a wave of all her waves
 But marks our English dead:
We have strawed our best to the weed's unrest,
 To the shark and the sheering gull.
If blood be the price of admiralty,
 Lord God, we ha' paid in full!

There's never a flood goes shoreward now
 But lifts a keel we manned;
There's never an ebb goes seaward now
 But drops our dead on the sand—
But slinks our dead on the sands forlore,
 From the Ducies to the Swin.[3]
If blood be the price of admiralty,
If blood be the price of admiralty,
 Lord God, we ha' paid it in!

We must feed our sea for a thousand years,
 For that is our doom and pride,
As it was when they sailed with the *Golden Hind,*
 Or the wreck that struck last tide—
Or the wreck that lies on the spouting reef
 Where the ghastly blue-lights flare.[4]
If blood be the price of admiralty,
If blood be the price of admiralty,
If blood be the price of admiralty,
 Lord God, we ha' bought it fair!

---

3. From Dulcie Island, in the central Pacific, to the Swin, which refers to one of the channels in the Thames Estuary in England.
4. Blue lights are used as a signal of distress at sea.

THE PALACE

When I was a King and a Mason—a Master proven and skilled—
I cleared me ground for a Palace such as a King should build.
I decreed and dug down to my levels. Presently, under the silt,
I came on the wreck of a Palace such as a King had built.

There was no worth in the fashion—there was no wit in the plan—
Hither and thither, aimless, the ruined footings ran—
Masonry, brute, mishandled, but carven on every stone:
"After me cometh a Builder. Tell him, I too have known."

Swift to my use in my trenches, where my well-planned ground-works
    grew,
I tumbled his quoins and his ashlars,[1] and cut and reset them anew.
Lime I milled of his marbles; burned it, slacked it, and spread;
Taking and leaving at pleasure the gifts of the humble dead.

Yet I despised not nor gloried; yet, as we wrenched them apart,
I read in the razed foundations the heart of that builder's heart.
As he had risen and pleaded, so did I understand
The form of the dream he had followed in the face of the thing he
    had planned.

✳✳✳

---

1. Quoins are cornerstones; ashlars are square-hewn stones.

When I was a King and a Mason—in the open noon of my pride,
They sent me a Word from the Darkness. They whispered and called
   me aside.
They said—"The end is forbidden." They said—"Thy use is fulfilled.
"Thy Palace shall stand as that other's—the spoil of a King who shall
   build."

I called my men from my trenches, my quarries, my wharves, and
   my sheers.[2]
All I had wrought I abandoned to the faith of the faithless years.
Only I cut on the timber—only I carved on the stone:
"After me cometh a Builder. Tell him, I too have known!"

---

2. Sheers are a device used to hoist up heavy items.

LETTING IN THE JUNGLE

Veil them, cover them, wall them round—
Blossom, and creeper, and weed—
Let us forget the sight and the sound,
The smell and the touch of the breed!

Fat black ash by the altar-stone,
Here is the white-foot rain
And the does bring forth in the fields unsown,
And none shall affright them again;
And the blind walls crumble, unknown, o'erthrown,
And none shall inhabit again!

CITIES AND THRONES AND POWERS

Cities and Thrones and Powers
  Stand in Time's eye,
Almost as long as flowers,
  Which daily die:
But, as new buds put forth
  To glad new men,
Out of the spent and unconsidered Earth
  The Cities rise again.

This season's Daffodil,
  She never hears
What change, what chance, what chill,
  Cut down last year's;
But with bold countenance,
  And knowledge small,
Esteems her seven days' continuance,
  To be perpetual.

So Time that is o'er-kind
  To all that be,
Ordains us e'en as blind,
  As bold as she:
That in our very death,
  And burial sure,
Shadow to shadow, well persuaded, saith,
  "See how our works endure!"

THE FOUR ANGELS

As Adam lay a-dreaming beneath the Apple Tree
The Angel of the Earth came down, and offered Earth in fee;
    But Adam did not need it,
    Nor the plough he would not speed it,
Singing:—"Earth and Water, Air and Fire,
    What more can mortal man desire?"
    (The Apple Tree's in bud.)

As Adam lay a-dreaming beneath the Apple Tree
The Angel of the Waters offered all the Seas in fee;
    But Adam would not take 'em,
    Nor the ships he wouldn't make 'em,
Singing:—"Water, Earth and Air and Fire,
    What more can mortal man desire?"
    (The Apple Tree's in leaf.)

As Adam lay a-dreaming beneath the Apple Tree
The Angel of the Air he offered all the Air in fee;
    But Adam did not crave it,
    Nor the flight he wouldn't brave it,
Singing:—"Air and Water, Earth and Fire,
    What more can mortal man desire?"
    (The Apple Tree's in bloom.)

As Adam lay a-dreaming beneath the Apple Tree
The Angel of the Fire rose up and not a word said he;
    But he wished a flame and made it,
    And in Adam's heart he laid it,
Singing:—"Fire, Fire, burning Fire!
    Stand up, and reach your heart's desire!"
    (The Apple Blossom's set.)

As Adam was a-working outside of Eden-Wall,
He used the Earth, he used the Seas, he used the Air and all;
    Till out of black disaster
    He arose to be a master
      Of Earth and Water, Air and Fire,
      But never reached his heart's desire!
      (The Apple Tree's cut down!)

IF

If you can keep your head when all about you[1]
  Are losing theirs and blaming it on you;
If you can trust yourself when all men doubt you,
  But make allowance for their doubting too:
If you can wait and not be tired by waiting,
  Or, being lied about, don't deal in lies,
Or being hated don't give way to hating,
  And yet don't look too good, nor talk too wise;

If you can dream—and not make dreams your master;
  If you can think—and not make thoughts your aim,
If you can meet with Triumph and Disaster
  And treat those two impostors just the same.
If you can bear to hear the truth you've spoken
  Twisted by knaves to make a trap for fools,
Or watch the things you gave your life to, broken,
  And stoop and build 'em up with worn-out tools;

If you can make one heap of all your winnings
  And risk it on one turn of pitch-and-toss,
And lose, and start again at your beginnings,
  And never breathe a word about your loss:
If you can force your heart and nerve and sinew
  To serve your turn long after they are gone,
And so hold on when there is nothing in you
  Except the Will which says to them: "Hold on!"

---

1. This poem was dedicated to Kipling's only son, Jack, who was twelve years old at the time of its writing. Jack was later killed in World War I.

If you can talk with crowds and keep your virtue,
   Or walk with Kings—nor lose the common touch,
If neither foes nor loving friends can hurt you,
   If all men count with you, but none too much:
If you can fill the unforgiving minute
   With sixty seconds' worth of distance run,
Yours is the Earth and everything that's in it,
   And—which is more—you'll be a Man, my son!

THE WAY THROUGH THE WOODS

They shut the road through the woods
  Seventy years ago.
Weather and rain have undone it again,
  And now you would never know
There was once a road through the woods
  Before they planted the trees.
It is underneath the coppice and heath,
  And the thin anemones.
  Only the keeper sees
That, where the ring-dove broods,
  And the badgers roll at ease,
There was once a road through the woods.

Yet, if you enter the woods
  Of a summer evening late,
When the night-air cools on the trout-ringed pools
  Where the otter whistles his mate.
(They fear not men in the woods,
  Because they see so few)
You will hear the beat of a horse's feet,
  And the swish of a skirt in the dew,
  Steadily cantering through
The misty solitudes,
  As though they perfectly knew
The old lost road through the woods. . . .
But there is no road through the woods!

THE WIDOWER

For a season there must be pain—
For a little, little space
I shall lose the sight of her face,
Take back the old life again
While She is at rest in her place.

For a season this pain must endure,
For a little, little while
I shall sigh more often than smile
Till time shall work me a cure,
And the pitiful days beguile.

For that season we must be apart,
For a little length of years,
Till my life's last hour nears,
And, above the beat of my heart,
I hear Her voice in my ears.

But I shall not understand—
Being set on some later love,
Shall not know her for whom I strove,
Till she reach me forth her hand,
Saying, "Who but I have the right?"
And out of a troubled night
Shall draw me safe to the land.

THE GLORY OF THE GARDEN

Our England is a garden that is full of stately views,
Of borders, beds and shrubberies and lawns and avenues,
With statues on the terraces and peacocks strutting by;
But the Glory of the Garden lies in more than meets the eye.

For where the old thick laurels grow, along the thin red wall,
You will find the tool- and potting-sheds which are the heart of all;
The cold-frames and the hot-houses, the dungpits and the tanks:
The rollers, carts and drain-pipes, with the barrows and the planks.

And there you'll see the gardeners, the men and 'prentice boys
Told off to do as they are bid and do it without noise;
For, except when seeds are planted and we shout to scare the birds,
The Glory of the Garden it abideth not in words.

And some can pot begonias and some can bud a rose,
And some are hardly fit to trust with anything that grows;
But they can roll and trim the lawns and sift the sand and loam,
For the Glory of the Garden occupieth all who come.

Our England is a garden, and such gardens are not made
By singing:—"Oh, how beautiful!" and sitting in the shade,
While better men than we go out and start their working lives
At grubbing weeds from gravel-paths with broken dinner-knives.

There's not a pair of legs so thin, there's not a head so thick,
There's not a hand so weak and white, nor yet a heart so sick.
But it can find some needful job that's crying to be done,
For the Glory of the Garden glorifieth every one.

Then seek your job with thankfulness and work till further orders,
If it's only netting strawberries or killing slugs on borders;
And when your back stops aching and your hands begin to harden,
You will find yourself a partner in the Glory of the Garden.

Oh, Adam was a gardener, and God who made him sees
That half a proper gardener's work is done upon his knees,
So when your work is finished, you can wash your hands and pray
For the Glory of the Garden, that it may not pass away!

And the Glory of the Garden it shall never pass away!

HERIOT'S FORD

"What's that that hirples[1] at my side?"
The foe that you must fight, my lord.
"That rides as fast as I can ride?"
The shadow of your might, my lord.

"Then wheel my horse against the foe!"
He's down and overpast, my lord.
You war against the sunset-glow,
The judgment follows fast, my lord!

"Oh, who will stay the sun's descent?"
King Joshua he is dead, my lord.
"I need an hour to repent!"
'Tis what our sister said, my lord.

"Oh, do not slay me in my sins!"
You're safe awhile with us, my lord.
"Nay, kill me ere my fear begins!"
We would not serve you thus, my lord.

"Where is the doom that I must face?"
Three little leagues away, my lord.
"Then mend the horses' laggard pace!"
We need them for next day, my lord.

"Next day—next day! Unloose my cords!"
Our sister needed none, my lord.
You had no mind to face our swords,
And—where can cowards run, my lord?

---

1. To run or walk as though lame.

"You would not kill the soul alive?"
'Twas thus our sister cried, my lord.
"I dare not die with none to shrive."
But so our sister died, my lord.

"Then wipe the sweat from brow and cheek."
It runnels forth afresh, my lord.
"Uphold me—for the flesh is weak."
You've finished with the Flesh, my lord!

"OUR FATHERS ALSO"

Thrones, Powers, Dominions, Peoples, Kings,
  Are changing 'neath our hand.
Our fathers also see these things
  But they do not understand.

By—they are by with mirth and tears,
  Wit or the works of Desire—
Cushioned about on the kindly years
  Between the wall and the fire.

The grapes are pressed, the corn is shocked—
  Standeth no more to glean;
For the Gates of Love and Learning locked
  When they went out between.

All lore our Lady Venus bares,
  Signalled it was or told
By the dear lips long given to theirs
  And longer to the mould.

All Profit, all Device, all Truth,
  Written it was or said
By the mighty men of their mighty youth,
  Which is mighty being dead.

The film that floats before their eyes
  The Temple's Veil they call;
And the dust that on the Shewbread lies
  Is holy over all.

Warn them of seas that slip our yoke,
  Of slow-conspiring stars—
The ancient Front of Things unbroke
  But heavy with new wars?

By—they are by with mirth and tears,
  Wit or the waste of Desire—
Cushioned about on the kindly years
  Between the wall and the fire!

THE FABULISTS

When all the world would keep a matter hid,
  Since Truth is seldom Friend to any crowd,
Men write in fable, as old Aesop did,
  Jesting at that which none will name aloud.
And this they needs must do, or it will fall
Unless they please they are not heard at all.

When desperate Folly daily laboureth
  To work confusion upon all we have,
When diligent Sloth demandeth Freedom's death,
  And banded Fear commandeth Honour's grave—
Even in that certain hour before the fall,
Unless men please they are not heard at all.

Needs must all please, yet some not all for need,
  Needs must all toil, yet some not all for gain,
But that men taking pleasure may take heed.
  Whom present toil shall snatch from later pain.
Thus some have toiled, but their reward was small
Since, though they pleased, they were not heard at all.

This was the lock that lay upon our lips,
  This was the yoke that we have undergone,
Denying us all pleasant fellowships
  As in our time and generation.
Our pleasures unpursued age past recall,
And for our pains—we are not heard at all.

What man hears aught except the groaning guns?
   What man heeds aught save what each instant brings?
When each man's life all imaged life outruns,
   What man shall pleasure in imaginings?
So it hath fallen, as it was bound to fall,
We are not, nor we were not, heard at all.

A DEATH-BED

"This is the State above the Law.
The State exists for the State alone."
*[This is a gland at the back of the jaw,
And an answering lump by the collarbone.]*[1]

Some die shouting in gas or fire;
Some die silent, by shell and shot.
Some die desperate, caught on the wire;
Some die suddenly. This will not.

"Regis suprema voluntas Lex"[2]
[It will follow the regular course of—throats.]
Some die pinned by the broken decks,
Some die sobbing between the boats.

Some die eloquent, pressed to death
By the sliding trench as their friends can hear.
Some die wholly in half a breath,
Some—give trouble for half a year.

"There is neither Evil nor Good in life
Except as the needs of the State ordain."
*[Since it is rather too late for the knife,
All we can do is mask the pain.]*

---

1. The deathbed is that of the former German kaiser, who was responsible for so many deaths in World War I. He was rumored to be dying from throat cancer. In actuality, the kaiser lived another twenty-two years cancer free.
2. "The will of the king is the supreme law."

Some die saintly in faith and hope—
One died thus in a prison-yard—
Some die broken by rape or the rope;
Some die easily. This dies hard.

"I will dash to pieces who bar my way.
Woe to the traitor! Woe to the weak!"
[Let him write what he wishes to say.
It tires him out if he tries to speak.]

Some die quietly. Some abound
In loud self-pity. Others spread
Bad morale through the cots around . . .
This is a type that is better dead.

"The war was forced on me by my foes.
All that I sought was the right to live."
[Don't be afraid of a triple dose;
The pain will neutralize half we give.

Here are the needles. See that he dies
While the effects of the drug endure . . .
What is the question he asks with his eyes?—
Yes, All-Highest, to God, be sure.]

ARITHMETIC ON THE FRONTIER

A great and glorious thing it is
  To learn, for seven years or so,
The Lord knows what of that and this,
  Ere reckoned fit to face the foe—
The flying bullet down the Pass,[1]
That whistles clear: "All flesh is grass."

Three hundred pounds per annum spent
  On making brain and body meeter
For all the murderous intent
  Comprised in "villanous saltpetre!"
And after—ask the Yusufzaies[2]
What comes of all our 'ologies.

A scrimmage in a Border Station—
  A canter down some dark defile—
Two thousand pounds of education
  Drops to a ten-rupee *jezail*[3]—
The Crammer's[4] boast, the Squadron's pride,
Shot like a rabbit in a ride!

---

1. Dangerous Khyber Pass, leading from India to Afghanistan.
2. A frontier tribe.
3. An Afghan musket.
4. A special school to prepare men for army service.

No proposition Euclid wrote,
  No formulae the text-books know,
Will turn the bullet from your coat,
  Or ward the tulwar's[5] downward blow
Strike hard who cares—shoot straight who can—
The odds are on the cheaper man.

One sword-knot[6] stolen from the camp
  Will pay for all the school expenses
Of any Kurrum Valley scamp[7]
  Who knows no word of moods and tenses,
But, being blessed with perfect sight,
Picks off our messmates left and right.

With home-bred hordes the hillsides teem,
  The troopships bring us one by one,
At vast expense of time and steam,
  To slay Afridis[8] where they run.
The "captives of our bow and spear"
Are cheap, alas! as we are dear.

---

5. An Indian saber.
6. A tassel tied to the hilt of a sword.
7. Native of the area along the border between Afghanistan and India (now Pakistan).
8. Another frontier tribe.

EN-DOR

"Behold there is a woman that hath a familiar spirit at En-dor."

—1 Samuel 28:7.

The road to En-dor is easy to tread
    For Mother or yearning Wife.
There, it is sure, we shall meet our Dead
    As they were even in life.
Earth has not dreamed of the blessing in store
For desolate hearts on the road to En-dor.

Whispers shall comfort us out of the dark—
    Hands—ah, God!—that we knew!
Visions and voices—look and hark!—
    Shall prove that the tale is true,
And that those who have passed to the further shore
May be hailed—at a price—on the road to En-dor.

But they are so deep in their new eclipse
    Nothing they say can reach,
Unless it be uttered by alien lips
    And I framed in a stranger's speech.
The son must send word to the mother that bore,
Through an hireling's mouth. 'Tis the rule of En-dor.

And not for nothing these gifts are shown
    By such as delight our dead.
They must twitch and stiffen and slaver and groan
    Ere the eyes are set in the head,
And the voice from the belly begins. Therefore,
We pay them a wage where they ply at En-dor.

Even so, we have need of faith
  And patience to follow the clue.
Often, at first, what the dear one saith
  Is babble, or jest, or untrue.
(Lying spirits perplex us sore
Till our loves—and their lives—are well-known at En-dor). . . .

Oh the road to En-dor is the oldest road
  And the craziest road of all!
Straight it runs to the Witch's abode,
  As it did in the days of Saul,
And nothing has changed of the sorrow in store
For such as go down on the road to En-dor!

BUTTERFLIES

Eyes aloft, over dangerous places,
The children follow the butterflies,
And, in the sweat of their upturned faces,
Slash with a net at the empty skies.

So it goes they fall amid brambles,
And sting their toes on the nettle-tops,
Till, after a thousand scratches and scrambles,
They wipe their brows and the hunting stops.

Then to quiet them comes their father
And stills the riot of pain and grief,
Saying, "Little ones, go and gather
Out of my garden a cabbage-leaf.

"You will find on it whorls and clots of
Dull grey eggs that, properly fed,
Turn, by way of the worm, to lots of
Glorious butterflies raised from the dead." . . .

"Heaven is beautiful, Earth is ugly,"
The three-dimensioned preacher saith;
So we must not look where the snail and the slug lie
For Psyche's birth. . . . And that is our death!

Natural Theology

PRIMITIVE

I ate my fill of a whale that died
  And stranded after a month at sea. . . .
There is a pain in my inside.
  Why have the Gods afflicted me?
Ow! I am purged till I am a wraith!
  Wow! I am sick till I cannot see!
What is the sense of Religion and Faith:
  Look how the Gods have afflicted me!

PAGAN

How can the skin of rat or mouse hold
  Anything more than a harmless flea? . . .
The burning plague has taken my household.
  Why have my Gods afflicted me?
All my kith and kin are deceased,
  Though they were as good as good could be,
I will out and batter the family priest,
  Because my Gods have afflicted me!

MEDIEVAL

My privy and well drain into each other
   After the custom of Christendie. . . .
Fevers and fluxes are wasting my mother.
   Why has the Lord afflicted me?
The Saints are helpless for all I offer—
   So are the clergy I used to fee.
Henceforward I keep my cash in my coffer,
   Because the Lord has afflicted me.

MATERIAL

I run eight hundred hens to the acre
   They die by dozens mysteriously. . . .
I am more than doubtful concerning my Maker,
   Why has the Lord afflicted me?
What a return for all my endeavour—
   Not to mention the L. S. D!¹
I am an atheist now and for ever,
   Because this God has afflicted me!

PROGRESSIVE

Money spent on an Army or Fleet
   Is homicidal lunacy. . . .
My son has been killed in the Mons retreat,²
   Why is the Lord afflicting me?
Why are murder, pillage and arson
   And rape allowed by the Deity?
I will write to the Times, deriding our parson
   Because my God has afflicted me.

---

1. L. S. D. is the abbreviation for the Latin *Libræ solidi denarii*, meaning "Pounds, shillings and pence."
2. The Mons retreat was a famous incident during World War I. Kipling's only son John actually died in another action during the war, at Loos in 1915.

CHORUS

We had a kettle: we let it leak:
   Our not repairing it made it worse.
We haven't had any tea for a week . . .
   The bottom is out of the Universe!

CONCLUSION

This was none of the good Lord's pleasure,
   For the Spirit He breathed in Man is free;
But what comes after is measure for measure,
   And not a God that afflicteth thee.
As was the sowing so the reaping
   Is now and evermore shall be.
Thou art delivered to thine own keeping.
   Only Thyself hath afflicted thee!

WHITE HORSES

Where run your colts at pasture?
Where hide your mares to breed?
'Mid bergs about the Ice-cap
    Or wove Sargasso weed;
By chartless reef and channel,
    Or crafty coastwise bars,
But most the ocean-meadows
    All purple to the stars!

Who holds the rein upon you?
    The latest gale let free.
What meat is in your mangers?
    The glut of all the sea.
'Twixt tide and tide's returning
    Great store of newly dead,—
The bones of those that faced us,
    And the hearts of those that fled.

Afar, off-shore and single,
    Some stallion, rearing swift,
Neighs hungry for new fodder,
    And calls us to the drift:
Then down the cloven ridges—
    A million hooves unshod—
Break forth the mad White Horses
    To seek their meat from God!

Girth-deep in hissing water
    Our furious vanguard strains—
Through mist of mighty tramplings
    Roll up the fore-blown manes—

A hundred leagues to leeward,
   Ere yet the deep is stirred,
The groaning rollers carry
   The coming of the herd!

Whose hand may grip your nostrils—
   Your forelock who may hold?
E'en they that use the broads with us—
   The riders bred and bold,
That spy upon our matings,
   That rope us where we run—
They know the strong White Horses
   From father unto son.

We breathe about their cradles,
   We race their babes ashore,
We snuff against their thresholds,
   We nuzzle at their door;
By day with stamping squadrons,
   By night in whinnying droves,
Creep up the wise White Horses,
   To call them from their loves.

And come they for your calling?
   No wit of man may save.
They hear the loosed White Horses
   Above their fathers' grave;
And, kin of those we crippled,
   And, sons of those we slew,
Spur down the wild white riders
   To school the herds anew.

What service have ye paid them,
   Oh jealous steeds and strong?
Save we that throw their weaklings,
   Is none dare work them wrong;
While thick around the homestead
   Our snow-backed leaders graze—
A guard behind their plunder,
   And a veil before their ways.

With march and countermarchings—
  With weight of wheeling hosts—
Stray mob or bands embattled—
  We ring the chosen coasts:
And, careless of our clamour
  That bids the stranger fly,
At peace within our pickets
  The wild white riders lie.

                    * * *

Trust ye that curdled hollows—
  Trust ye the neighing wind—
Trust ye the moaning groundswell—
  Our herds are close behind!
To bray your foeman's armies—
  To chill and snap his sword—
Trust ye the wild White Horses,
  The Horses of the Lord!

THE OLDEST SONG

"For before Eve was Lilith."
—*Old Tale.*

"These were never your true love's eyes.
  Why do you feign that you love them?
You that broke from their constancies,
  And the wide calm brows above them!

This was never your true love's speech.
  Why do you thrill when you hear it?
You that have ridden out of its reach
  The width of the world or near it!

This was never your true love's hair,—
  You that chafed when it bound you
Screened from knowledge or shame or care,
  In the night that it made around you!"

"All these things I know, I know.
  And that's why my heart is breaking!"
"Then what do you gain by pretending so?"
  "The joy of an old wound waking."

THE OLD MEN

This is our lot if we live so long and labour unto the end—
Then we outlive the impatient years and the much too patient friend:
And because we know we have breath in our mouth and think we have
  thoughts enough in our head,
We shall assume that we are alive, whereas we are really dead.

We shall not acknowledge that old stars fade or stronger planets arise
(That the sere bush buds or the desert blooms or the ancient well-
  head dries),
Or any new compass wherewith new men adventure 'neath new skies.

We shall lift up the ropes that constrained our youth, to bind on our
  children's hands;
We shall call to the waters below the bridges to return and to replenish
  our lands;
We shall harness horses (Death's own pale horses) and scholarly plough
  the sands.

We shall lie down in the eye of the sun for lack of a light on our way—
We shall rise up when the day is done and chirrup, "Behold, it is day!"
We shall abide till the battle is won ere we amble into the fray.

We shall peck out and discuss and dissect, and evert[1] and extrude
  to our mind,
The flaccid tissues of long-dead issues offensive to God and mankind—
(Precisely like vultures over an ox that the army left behind).

---

1. Turn inside out.

We shall make walk preposterous ghosts of the glories we once
created—
Immodestly smearing from muddled palettes amazing pigments
mismated—
And our friends will weep when we ask them with boasts if our natural
force be abated.

The Lamp of our Youth will be utterly out, but we shall subsist on
the smell of it;
And whatever we do, we shall fold our hands and suck our gums and
think well of it.
Yes, we shall be perfectly pleased with our work, and that is the
Perfectest Hell of it!

This is our lot if we live so long and listen to those who love us—
That we are shunned by the people about and shamed by the Powers
above us.
Wherefore be free of your harness betimes; but, being free be assured,
That he who hath not endured to the death, from his birth he hath never
endured!

Part IV

GOVERNMENT AND POLITICS

THE HOUSES

(*A Song of the Dominions*)

'Twixt my house and thy house the pathway is broad,
In thy house or my house is half the world's hoard;
By my house and thy house hangs all the world's fate,
On thy house and my house lies half the world's hate.

For my house and thy house no help shall we find
Save thy house and my house—kin cleaving to kind;
If my house be taken, thine tumbleth anon.
If thy house be forfeit, mine followeth soon.

'Twixt my house and thy house what talk can there be
Of headship or lordship, or service or fee?
Since my house to thy house no greater can send
Than thy house to my house—friend comforting friend;
And thy house to my house no meaner can bring
Than my house to thy house—King counselling King!

THE HERITAGE

Our Fathers in a wondrous age,
  Ere yet the Earth was small,
Ensured to us a heritage,
  And doubted not at all
That we the children of their heart,
  Which then did beat so high,
In later rime should play like part
  For our posterity.

A thousand years they steadfast built,
  To 'vantage us and ours,
The Walls that were a world's despair,
  The sea-constraining Towers:
Yet in their midmost pride they knew,
  And unto Kings made known,
Not all from these their strength they drew,
  Their faith from brass or stone.

Youth's passion, manhood's fierce intent,
  With age's judgment wise,
They spent, and counted not they spent,
  At daily sacrifice.
Not lambs alone nor purchased doves.
  Or tithe of trader's gold—
Their lives most dear, their dearer loves,
  They offered up of old.

Refraining e'en from lawful things,
  They bowed the neck to bear
The unadorned yoke that brings
  Stark toil and sternest care.
Wherefore through them is Freedom sure;
  Wherefore through them we stand,
From all but sloth and pride secure,
  In a delightsome land.

Then, fretful, murmur not they gave
  So great a charge to keep,
Nor dream that awestruck Time shall save
  Their labour while we sleep.
Dear-bought and clear, a thousand year,
  Our fathers' title runs.
Make we likewise their sacrifice,
  Defrauding not our sons.

THE RUPAIYAT OF OMAR KAL'VIN

[Allowing for the difference 'twixt prose and rhymed exaggeration, this ought to reproduce the sense of what Sir Auckland (Colvin) told the nation some time ago, when the Government struck from our incomes two per cent.][1]

Now the New Year, reviving last Year's Debt,
The Thoughtful Fisher casteth wide his Net;
    So I with begging Dish and ready Tongue
Assail all Men for all that I can get.

Imports indeed are gone with all their Dues—
Lo! Salt a Lever that I dare not use,
    Nor may I ask the Tillers in Bengal—
Surely my Kith and Kin will not refuse!

Pay—and I promise by the Dust of Spring,
Retrenchment. If my promises can bring
    Comfort, Ye have Them now a thousandfold—
By Allah! I will promise Anything!

Indeed, indeed, Retrenchment oft before
I swore—but did I mean it when I swore?
    And then, and then, We wandered to the Hills,
And so the Little Less became Much More.

---

1. A Kipling scholar wrote, "This poem is a parody [Edward] Fitzgerald's now famous translation of "The Rubaiyat of Omar Khayyan." A "Rubaiyat" is a poem and a "rupiya" is a rupee, the standard coin in India" (Ralph Durand, *A Handbook to the Poetry of Rudyard Kipling,* 1914). This poem was written in protest of an increase in the income tax in India, which was levied by Sir Auckland Colvin, who was in charge of the finances in the northwest provinces of India.

Whether a Boileaugunge or Babylon,[2]
I know not how the wretched Thing is done,
    The Items of Receipt grow surely small;
The Items of Expense mount one by one.

I cannot help it. What have I to do
With One and Five, or Four, or Three, or Two?
    Let Scribes spit Blood and Sulphur as they please,
Or Statesmen call me foolish—Heed not you.

Behold, I promise—Anything You will.
Behold, I greet you with an empty Till—
    Ah! Fellow-Sinners, of your Charity
Seek not the Reason of the Dearth, but fill.

For if I sinned and fell, where lies the Gain
Of Knowledge? Would it ease you of your Pain
    To know the tangled Threads of Revenue,
I ravel deeper in a hopeless Skein?

"Who hath not Prudence"—what was it I said,
Of Her who paints her Eyes and tires Her Head,
    And gibes and mocks the People in the Street,
And fawns upon them for Her thriftless Bread?

Accursed is She of Eve's daughters—She
Hath cast off Prudence, and Her End shall be
    Destruction . . . Brethren, of your Bounty grant
Some Portion of your daily Bread to *Me!*

---

2. Boileaugunge is a suburb of Simla, the summer capital of British India. Babylon, symbolic for unrighteous seat of government, is mentioned in stanza 8 of Fitzgerald's "Rubaiyat."

THE OLD ISSUE

(Outbreak of Boer War)

October 9, 1899

"Here is nothing new nor aught unproven," say the Trumpets,
"Many feet have worn it and the road is old indeed.
It is the King—the King we schooled aforetime!"
(Trumpets in the marshes—in the eyot at Runnymede!)

"Here is neither haste, nor hate, nor anger," peal the Trumpets,
"Pardon for his penitence or pity for his fall.
It is the King!"—inexorable Trumpets—
(Trumpets round the scaffold at the dawning by Whitehall!)

***

"He hath veiled the Crown and hid the Scepter," warn the Trumpets,
"He hath changed the fashion of the lies that cloak his will.
Hard die the Kings—ah hard—dooms hard!" declare the Trumpets,
Trumpets at the gang-plank where the brawling troop-decks fill!

Ancient and Unteachable, abide—abide the Trumpets!
Once again the Trumpets, for the shuddering ground-swell brings
Clamour over ocean of the harsh, pursuing Trumpets—
Trumpets of the Vanguard that have sworn no truce with Kings!

All we have of freedom, all we use or know—
This our fathers bought for us long and long ago.

Ancient Right unnoticed as the breath we draw—
Leave to live by no man's leave, underneath the Law.

Lance and torch and tumult, steel and grey-goose wing
Wrenched it, inch and ell and all, slowly from the king.

Till our fathers 'stablished, after bloody years,
How our King is one with us, first among his peers.

So they bought us freedom—not at little cost—
Wherefore must we watch the King, lest our gain be lost.

Over all things certain, this is sure indeed,
Suffer not the old King: for we know the breed.

Give no ear to bondsmen bidding us endure.
Whining "He is weak and far"; crying "Time will cure."

(Time himself is witness, till the battle joins,
Deeper strikes the rottenness in the people's loins.)

Give no heed to bondsmen masking war with peace.
Suffer not the old King here or overseas.

They that beg us barter—wait his yielding mood—
Pledge the years we hold in trust—pawn our brother's blood—

Howso' great their clamour, whatsoe'er their claim,
Suffer not the old King under any name!

Here is naught unproven—here is naught to learn.
It is written what shall fall if the King return.

He shall mark our goings, question whence we came,
Set his guards about us, as in Freedom's name.

He shall take a tribute, toll of all our ware;
He shall change our gold for arms—arms we may not bear.

He shall break his Judges if they cross his word;
He shall rule above the Law calling on the Lord.

He shall peep and mutter; and the night shall bring
Watchers 'neath our window, lest we mock the King—

Hate and all division; hosts of hurrying spies;
Money poured in secret, carrion breeding flies.

Strangers of his counsel, hirelings of his pay,
These shall deal our Justice: sell—deny—delay.

We shall drink dishonour, we shall eat abuse
For the Land we look to—for the Tongue we use.

We shall take our station, dirt beneath his feet,
While his hired captains jeer us in the street.

Cruel in the shadow, crafty in the sun,
Far beyond his borders shall his teachings run.

Sloven, sullen, savage, secret, uncontrolled,
Laying on a new land evil of the old—

Long-forgotten bondage, dwarfing heart and brain—
All our fathers died to loose he shall bind again.

Here is naught at venture, random nor untrue
Swings the wheel full-circle, brims the cup anew.

Here is naught unproven, here is nothing hid:
Step for step and word for word—so the old Kings did!

Step by step, and word by word: who is ruled may read.
Suffer not the old Kings: for we know the breed—

All the right they promise—all the wrong they bring.
Stewards of the Judgment, suffer not this King!

THE KINGDOM

Now we are come to our Kingdom,
  And the State is thus and thus;
Our legions wait at the Palace gate—
  Little it profits us.
    Now we are come to our Kingdom!

Now we are come to our Kingdom,
  And the Crown is ours to take—
With a naked sword at the Council board,
  And under the throne the snake.
    Now we are come to our Kingdom!

Now we are come for our Kingdom,
  And the Realm is ours by right,
With shame and fear for our daily cheer,
  And heaviness at night.
    Now we are come to our Kingdom!

Now we are come to our Kingdom,
  But my love's eyelids fall.
All that I wrought for, all that I fought for,
  Delight her nothing at all.
  My crown is of withered leaves,
  For she sits in the dust and grieves.
    Now we are come for our Kingdom!

A PICT SONG

Rome never looks where she treads.
  Always her heavy hooves fall
On our stomachs, our hearts or our heads;
  And Rome never heeds when we bawl.
Her sentries pass on—that is all,
  And we gather behind them in hordes,
And plot to reconquer the Wall,
  With only our tongues for our swords.

We are the Little Folk—we!
  Too little to love or to hate.
Leave us alone and you'll see
  How we can drag down the State!
We are the worm in the wood!
  We are the rot at the root!
We are the taint in the blood!
  We are the thorn in the foot!

Mistletoe killing an oak—
  Rats gnawing cables in two—
Moths making holes in a cloak—
  How they must love what they do!
Yes—and we Little Folk too,
  We are busy as they—
Working our works out of view—
  Watch, and you'll see it someday!

No indeed! We are not strong,
   But we know Peoples that are.
Yes, and we'll guide them along
   To smash and destroy you in War!
We shall be slaves just the same?
   Yes, we have always been slaves,
But you—you will die of the shame,
   And then we shall dance on your graves!

We are the Little Folk, we, etc.

THE STRANGER

The Stranger within my gate,
  He may be true or kind,
But he does not talk my talk—
  I cannot feel his mind.
I see the face and the eyes and the mouth,
  But not the soul behind.

The men of my own stock,
  They may do ill or well,
But they tell the lies I am wonted to,
  They are used to the lies I tell;
And we do not need interpreters
  When we go to buy or sell.

The Stranger within my gates,
  He may be evil or good,
But I cannot tell what powers control—
  What reasons sway his mood;
Nor when the Gods of his far-off land
  Shall repossess his blood.

The men of my own stock,
  Bitter bad they may be,
But, at least, they hear the things I hear,
  And see the things I see;
And whatever I think of them and their likes
  They think of the likes of me.

This was my father's belief
  And this is also mine:
Let the corn be all one sheaf—
  And the grapes be all one vine,
Ere our children's teeth are set on edge
  By bitter bread and wine.

MY FATHER'S CHAIR

Parliaments of Henry III, 1265

There are four good legs to my Father's Chair—
  Priests and People and Lords and Crown.
I sits on all of 'em fair and square,
  And that is the reason it don't break down.

I won't trust one leg, nor two, nor three,
  To carry my weight when I sets me down.
I wants all four of 'em under me—
  Priests and People and Lords and Crown.

I sits on all four and favours none—
  Priests, nor People, nor Lords, nor Crown:
And I never tilts in my chair, my son,
  And that is the reason it don't break down.

When your time comes to sit in my Chair,
  Remember your Father's habits and rules,
Sit on all four legs, fair and square,
  And never be tempted by one-legged stools!

THE COVENANT

We thought we ranked above the chance of ill.[1]
 Others might fall, not we, for we were wise—
Merchants in freedom. So, of our free-will
 We let our servants drug our strength with lies.
The pleasure and the poison had its way
 On us as on the meanest, till we learned
That he who lies will steal, who steals will slay.
 Neither God's judgment nor man's heart was turned.

Yet there remains His Mercy—to be sought
Through wrath and peril till we cleanse the wrong
By that last right which our forefathers claimed
When their Law failed them and its stewards were bought.
This is our cause. God help us, and make strong
Our wills to meet Him later, unashamed!

---

1. "The Covenant" was written during a time when many Irish were seeking Home Rule, rather than being governed by Great Britain. Civil war threatened. Kipling warned against lying politicians and encouraged the Irish to fight for their freedom.

THE DECLARATION OF LONDON

June 29, 1911

On the reassembling of Parliament after the Coronation, the Government have no intention of allowing their followers to vote according to their convictions on the Declaration of London, but insist on a strictly party vote.—Daily Papers

We were all one heart and one race
  When the Abbey trumpets blew.[1]
For a moment's breathing-space
  We had forgotten you.[2]
Now you return to your honoured place
  Panting to shame us anew.

We have walked with the Ages dead—
  With our Past alive and ablaze.
And you bid us pawn our honour for bread,
  This day of all the days!
And you cannot wait till our guests are sped,
  Or last week's wreath decays?

---

1. This is a reference to the coronation of George V of England.
2. The "you" refers to parliament, which voted along party lines to support or defeat the Declaration of London. That declaration was designed to prescribe the regulation of shipping in wartime. Had it passed, it would have been harmful to the interests of Britain.

The light is still in our eyes
　Of Faith and Gentlehood,
Of Service and Sacrifice;
　And it does not match our mood,
To turn so soon to your treacheries
　That starve our land of her food.

Our ears still carry the sound
　Of our once-Imperial seas,
Exultant after our King was crowned,
　Beneath the sun and the breeze.
It is too early to have them bound
　Or sold at your decrees.

Wait till the memory goes,
　Wait till the visions fade,
We may betray in time, God knows,
　But we would not have it said,
When you make report to our scornful foes,
　That we kissed as we betrayed!

GEHAZI

"Whence comest thou, Gehazi,[1]
  So reverend to behold,
In scarlet and in ermines
  And chain of England's gold?"
"From following after Naaman
  To tell him all is well,
Whereby my zeal hath made me
  A Judge in Israel."

Well done; well done, Gehazi!
  Stretch forth thy ready hand,
Thou barely 'scaped from judgment,
  Take oath to judge the land
Unswayed by gift of money
  Or privy bribe, more base,
Of knowledge which is profit
  In any market-place.

Search out and probe, Gehazi,
  As thou of all canst try,
The truthful, well-weighed answer
  That tells the blacker lie—
The loud, uneasy virtue
  The anger feigned at will,
To overbear a witness
  And make the Court keep still.

---

1. See Holy Bible, 2 Kings 5:25; see also Julian Moore, "Gehazi," at http://www.kiplingsociety.co.uk/rg_gehazi_moore.htm. This poem condemns government officials who use their offices for personal gain.

Take order now, Gehazi,
    That no man talk aside
In secret with his judges
    The while his case is tried.
Lest he should show them—reason
    To keep a matter hid,
And subtly lead the questions
    Away from what he did.

Thou mirror of uprightness,
    What ails thee at thy vows?
What means the risen whiteness
    Of the skin between thy brows?
The boils that shine and burrow,
    The sores that slough and bleed—
The leprosy of Naaman
    On thee and all thy seed?
        Stand up, stand up, Gehazi,
            Draw close thy robe and go,
        Gehazi, Judge in Israel,
            A leper white as snow!

MACDONOUGH'S SONG

Whether the State can loose and bind
  In Heaven as well as on Earth:
If it be wiser to kill mankind
  Before or after the birth—
These are matters of high concern
  Where State-kept schoolmen are;
But Holy State (we have lived to learn)
  Endeth in Holy War.

Whether The People be led by The Lord,
  Or lured by the loudest throat:
If it be quicker to die by the sword
  Or cheaper to die by vote—
These are things we have dealt with once,
  (And they will not rise from their grave)
For Holy People, however it runs,
  Endeth in wholly Slave.

Whatsoever, for any cause,
  Seeketh to take or give
Power above or beyond the Laws,
  Suffer it not to live!
Holy State or Holy King—
  Or Holy People's Will—
Have no truck with the senseless thing.
  Order the guns and kill!
    Saying—after—me:—

Once there was The People—Terror gave it birth;
Once there was The People and it made a Hell of Earth.
Earth arose and crushed it. Listen, O ye slain!
Once there was The People—it shall never be again!

SEVEN WATCHMEN

Seven Watchmen sitting in a tower,
  Watching what had come upon mankind,
Showed the Man the Glory and the Power,
  And bade him shape the Kingdom to his mind.
"All things on Earth your will shall win you."
  ('Twas so their counsel ran)
"But the Kingdom—the Kingdom is within you,"
  Said the Man's own mind to the Man.
    For time—and some time—
As it was in the bitter years before
  So it shall be in the over-sweetened hour—
That a man's mind is wont to tell him more
  Than Seven Watchmen sitting in a tower.

A DEAD STATESMAN

I could not dig; I dared not rob:
Therefore I lied to please the mob.
Now all my lies are proved untrue
And I must face the men I slew.
What tale shall serve me here among
Mine angry and defrauded young?

Part V

WAR AND PEACE

HYMN BEFORE ACTION

The earth is full of anger,
  The seas are dark with wrath,
The Nations in their harness
  Go up against our path:
Ere yet we loose the legions—
  Ere yet we draw the blade,
Jehovah of the Thunders,
  Lord God of Battles, aid!

High lust and froward bearing,
  Proud heart, rebellious brow—
Deaf ear and soul uncaring,
  We seek Thy mercy now!
The sinner that forswore Thee,
  The fool that passed Thee by,
Our times are known before Thee—
  Lord, grant us strength to die!

For those who kneel beside us
  At altars not Thine own,
Who lack the lights that guide us,
  Lord, let their faith atone!
If wrong we did to call them,
  By honour bound they came;
Let not Thy Wrath befall them,
  But deal to us the blame.

From panic, pride, and terror
  Revenge that knows no rein—
Light haste and lawless error,
  Protect us yet again,
Cloke Thou our undeserving,
  Make firm the shuddering breath,
In silence and unswerving
  To taste Thy lesser death.

Ah, Mary pierced with sorrow,
  Remember, reach and save
The soul that comes tomorrow
  Before the God that gave!
Since each was born of woman,
  For each at utter need—
True comrade and true foeman—
  Madonna, intercede!

E'en now their vanguard gathers,
  E'en now we face the fray—
As Thou didst help our fathers,
  Help Thou our host today.
Fulfilled of signs and wonders,
  In life, in death made clear—
Jehovah of the Thunders,
  Lord God of Battles, hear!

THE VETERANS

*Written for the Gathering of Survivors the Indian Mutiny,
Albert Hall, 1907*[1]

Today, across our fathers' graves,
The astonished years reveal
The remnant of that desperate host
Which cleansed our East with steel.

Hail and farewell! We greet you here,
With tears that none will scorn—
O Keepers of the House of old,
Or ever we were born!

One service more we dare to ask—
Pray for us, heroes, pray,
That when Fate lays on us our task
We do not shame the Day!

---

1. During the British occupation of India, British authorities sent 50,000 troops to keep order in the country. British officers also commanded 300,000 native Indian soldiers. In May 1857, the Indian soldiers rose up in mutiny against the British overlords. This uprising is variously known as "The Sepoy Rebellion," "The Great Rebellion," "The Revolt of 1857," and "India's First War of Independence." The brutality on both sides was shocking. The death toll among the Indians eventually rose to more than 100,000 (including many who were not involved in the rebellion), while the British lost some 11,000 men. Kipling was born in Bombay only seven years after the end of the rebellion, and from time to time he wrote about its atrocities. This poem was written for a memorial that was held in England fifty years after the beginning of the rebellion. The "survivors" mentioned in the headnote were British soldiers.

JUBAL AND TUBAL CAIN

Jubal sang of the Wrath of God
  And the curse of thistle and thorn—
But Tubal got him a pointed rod,
  And scrabbled the earth for corn.
Old—old as that early mould,
  Young as the sprouting grain—
Yearly green is the strife between
  Jubal and Tubal Cain!¹

Jubal sang of the new-found sea,
  And the love that its waves divide—
But Tubal hollowed a fallen tree
  And passed to the further side.
Black—black as the hurricane-wrack,
  Salt as the under-main—
Bitter and cold is the hate they hold—
  Jubal and Tubal Cain!

Jubal sang of the golden years
  When wars and wounds shall cease—
But Tubal fashioned the hand-flung spears
  And showed his neighbours peace.

---

1. Jubal and Tubal-Cain were half-brothers, descendants of Cain, the son of Adam and Eve. Their father was Lamech, mentioned in the third stanza (see Genesis 4:17-22). Jubal was "the father of all who play stringed instruments and pipes." Tubal-Cain "forged all kinds of tools out of bronze and iron" (see Genesis 4:21-22 NIV).

New—new as Nine-point-Two,
 Older than Lamech's slain[2]—
Roaring and loud is the feud avowed
 Twix' Jubal and Tubal Cain!

Jubal sang of the cliffs that bar
 And the peaks that none may crown—
But Tubal clambered by jut and scar
 And there he builded a town.
 High—high as the snowsheds lie,
  Low as the culverts drain—
 Wherever they be they can never agree—
  Jubal and Tubal Cain!

---

2. Lamech boasted that he killed a man (see Genesis 4:23-24).

THE PIRATES IN ENGLAND

(Saxon Invasion, A.D. 400–600)

When Rome was rotten-ripe to her fall,
  And the sceptre passed from her hand,
The pestilent Picts leaped over the wall
  To harry the English land.

The little dark men of the mountain and waste,
  So quick to laughter and tears,
They came panting with hate and haste
  For the loot of five hundred years.

They killed the trader, they sacked the shops,
  They ruined temple and town—
They swept like wolves through the standing crops
  Crying that Rome was down.

They wiped out all that they could find
  Of beauty and strength and worth,
But they could not wipe out the Viking's Wind
  That brings the ships from the North.

They could not wipe out the North-East gales
  Nor what those gales set free—
The pirate ships with their close-reefed sails,
  Leaping from sea to sea.

They had forgotten the shield-hung hull
  Seen nearer and more plain,
Dipping into the troughs like a gull,
  And gull-like rising again—

The painted eyes that glare and frown
  In the high snake-headed stem,
Searching the beach while her sail comes down,
  They had forgotten them!

There was no Count of the Saxon Shore
  To meet her hand to hand,
As she took the beach with a grind and a roar,
  And the pirates rushed inland!

"For All We Have and Are"

For all we have and are,
For all our children's fate,
Stand up and take the war.
The Hun is at the gate!
Our world has passed away,
In wantonness o'erthrown.
There is nothing left today
But steel and fire and stone!
  Though all we knew depart,
  The old Commandments stand:—
  "In courage keep your heart,
  In strength lift up your hand."

Once more we hear the word
That sickened earth of old:—
"No law except the Sword
Unsheathed and uncontrolled."
Once more it knits mankind,
Once more the nations go
To meet and break and bind
A crazed and driven foe.

Comfort, content, delight,
The ages' slow-bought gain,
They shrivelled in a night.
Only ourselves remain

To face the naked days
In silent fortitude,
Through perils and dismays
Renewed and re-renewed.
    Though all we made depart,
    The old Commandments stand:—
    "In patience keep your heart,
    In strength lift up your hand."

No easy hope or lies
Shall bring us to our goal,
But iron sacrifice
Of body, will, and soul.
There is but one task for all—
One life for each to give.
What stands if Freedom fall?
Who dies if England live?

THE GRAVE OF THE HUNDRED HEAD

There's a widow in sleepy Chester[1]
Who weeps for her only son;
There's a grave on the Pabeng River,[2]
A grave that the Burmans shun;
And there's Subadar[3] *Prag Tewarri*
Who tells how the work was done.

A Snider[4] squibbed in the jungle,
 Somebody laughed and fled,
And the men of the First Shikaris[5]
 Picked up their Subaltern[6] dead,
With a big blue mark in his forehead
 And the back blown out of his head.

Subadar Prag Tewarri,
 Jemadar[7] Hira Lal,
Took command of the party,
 Twenty rifles in all,
Marched them down to the river
 As the day was beginning to fall.

---

1. A city in Cheshire, England.
2. Except for Chester, the locations in the poem are in Upper Burma, now known as Myanmar. The British annexed Upper Burma in 1886, a move that was resisted by Burmese guerrillas.
3. The chief native officer over a company of soldiers in the Indian army, which fought under British direction.
4. A rifle invented by an American named Jacob Snider; it was adopted by the British army.
5. An imaginary army regiment.
6. An officer below the rank of captain in the British army.
7. In the Indian army, a second native officer with authority just below that of Subadar.

142

They buried the boy by the river,
  A blanket over his face—
They wept for their dead Lieutenant,
  The men of an alien race—
They made a *samadh*[8] in his honor,
  A mark for his resting-place.

For they swore by the Holy Water,
  They swore by the salt they ate,
That the soul of Lieutenant Eshmitt Sahib
  Should go to his God in state,
With fifty file[9] of Burmans
  To open him Heaven's gate.

The men of the First Shikaris
  Marched till the break of day,
Till they came to the rebel village,
  The village of Pabengmay—
A *jingal*[10] covered the clearing,
  Calthrops[11] hampered the way.

Subadar Prag Tewarri,
  Bidding them load with ball,
Halted a dozen rifles
  Under the village wall;
Sent out a flanking-party
  With Jemadar Hira Lal.

The men of the First Shikaris
  Shouted and smote and slew,
Turning the grinning *jingal*
  On to the howling crew.
The Jemadar's flanking-party
  Butchered the folk who flew.

---

8. A memorial.
9. One hundred soldiers marching in ranks of two.
10. A cannon.
11. Iron spikes.

Long was the morn of slaughter,
  Long was the list of slain,
Five score heads were taken,
  Five score heads and twain;
And the men of the First Shikaris
  Went back to their grave again,

Each man bearing a basket
  Red as his palms that day,
Red as the blazing village—
  The village of Pabengmay,
And the *"drip-drip-drip"* from the baskets
  Reddened the grass by the way.

They made a pile of their trophies
  High as a tall man's chin,
Head upon head distorted,
  Set in a sightless grin,
Anger and pain and terror
  Stamped on the smoke-scorched skin.

Subadar Prag Tewarri
  Put the head of the Boh[12]
On the top of the mound of triumph,
  The head of his son below—
With the sword and the peacock-banner
  That the world might behold and know.

Thus the *samadh* was perfect,
  Thus was the lesson plain
Of the wrath of the First Shikaris—
  The price of a white man slain;
And the men of the First Shikaris
  Went back into camp again.

---

12. Leader of a band of Burmese rebels.

Then a silence came to the river,
  A hush fell over the shore,
And Bohs that were brave departed,
  And Sniders squibbed no more;
    For the Burmans said
    That a white man's head
Must be paid for with heads five-score.

There's a widow in sleepy Chester
  Who weeps for her only son;
There's a grave on the Pabeng River,
  A grave that the Burmans shun;
And there's Subadar Prag Tewarri
  Who tells how the work was done.

GENTLEMAN-RANKERS

To the legion of the lost ones, to the cohort of the damned,
  To my brethren in their sorrow overseas,
Sings a gentleman of England cleanly bred, machinely crammed,[1]
  And a trooper of the Empress, if you please.
Yea, a trooper of the forces who has run his own six horses,
  And faith he went the pace and went it blind,
And the world was more than kin while he held the ready tin,
  But today the Sergeant's something less than kind.
      We're poor little lambs who've lost our way,
        Baa! Baa! Baa!
      We're little black sheep who've gone astray,
        Baa—aa—aa!
      Gentlemen-rankers out on the spree,
      Damned from here to Eternity,
      God ha' mercy on such as we,
        Baa! Yah! Bah!

Oh, it's sweet to sweat through stables, sweet to empty kitchen slops,
  And it's sweet to hear the tales the troopers tell,
To dance with blowzy housemaids at the regimental hops
  And thrash the cad who says you waltz too well.
Yes, it makes you cock-a-hoop[2] to be "Rider" to your troop,[3]
  And branded with a blasted worsted spur,
When you envy, O how keenly, one poor Tommy[4] being cleanly
  Who blacks your boots and sometimes calls you "Sir."

---

1. Gentlemen-rankers are educated but poor men who join the army, as enlisted men, as a way to make a living.
2. Proud and loud.
3. The "rider" trained the most difficult horses.
4. Common soldier.

If the home we never write to, and the oaths we never keep,
  And all we know most distant and most dear,
Across the snoring barrack-room return to break our sleep,
  Can you blame us if we soak ourselves in beer?
When the drunken comrade mutters and the great guard-lantern gutters
  And the horror of our fall is written plain,
Every secret, self-revealing on the aching white-washed ceiling,
  Do you wonder that we drug ourselves from pain?

We have done with Hope and Honour, we are lost to Love and Truth,
  We are dropping down the ladder rung by rung,
And the measure of our torment is the measure of our youth.
  God help us, for we knew the worst too young!
Our shame is clean repentance for the crime that brought the sentence,
  Our pride it is to know no spur of pride,
And the Curse of Reuben[5] holds us till an alien turf enfolds us
  And we die, and none can tell Them where we died.
    We're poor little lambs who've lost our way,
      Baa! Baa! Baa!
    We're little black sheep who've gone astray,
      Baa—aa—aa!
    Gentlemen-rankers out on the spree,
    Damned from here to Eternity,
    God ha' mercy on such as we,
      Baa! Yah! Bah!

---

5. Reuben, one of the twelve sons of Jacob, was cursed that he would never excel (see Genesis 49:4).

THE ISLANDERS

No doubt but ye are the People[1]*—your throne is above the King's.*
Whoso speaks in your presence must say acceptable things:
Bowing the head in worship, bending the knee in fear—
Bringing the word well smoothen—such as a King should hear.

Fenced by your careful fathers, ringed by your leaden seas,
Long did ye wake in quiet and long lie down at ease;
Till ye said of Strife: "What is it?" Of the Sword: "It is far from our ken";
Till ye made a sport of your shrunken hosts and a toy of your armed men.

Ye stopped your ears to the warning—ye would neither look nor heed—
Ye set your leisure before their toil and your lusts above their need.
Because of your witless learning and your beasts of warren and chase,
Ye grudged your sons to their service and your fields for their camping-place.[2]
Ye forced them glean in the highways the straw for the bricks they brought;[3]
Ye forced them follow in byways the craft that ye never taught.
Ye hampered and hindered and crippled; ye thrust out of sight and away
Those that would serve you for honour and those that served you for pay.

---

1. This is Job's jab at those who falsely thought they had the greatest wisdom; see Job 12:2.
2. With no fear of war, the English did not want their sons to join military service, nor did they want their lands to be used for training of troops.
3. See Exodus 5:7. The English placed impossible demands on the military without providing the necessary resources.

148

Then were the judgments loosened; then was your shame revealed,
At the hands of a little people, few but apt in the field.
Yet ye were saved by a remnant (and your land's long-suffering star),
When your strong men cheered in their millions while your striplings
    went to the war.
Sons of the sheltered city—unmade, unhandled, unmeet—[4]
Ye pushed them raw to the battle as ye picked them raw from the street.
And what did ye look they should compass? Warcraft learned in a
    breath,
Knowledge unto occasion at the first far view of Death?
So? And ye train your horses and the dogs ye feed and prize?
How are the beasts more worthy than the souls, your sacrifice?
But ye said, "Their valour shall show them"; but ye said, "The end
    is close."
And ye sent them comfits and pictures to help them harry your foes:[5]
And ye vaunted your fathomless power, and ye flaunted your iron pride,
Ere ye fawned on the Younger Nations for the men who could shoot
    and ride![6]
Then ye returned to your trinkets; then ye contented your souls
With the flannelled fools at the wicket or the muddied oafs at the goals.[7]
Given to strong delusion, wholly believing a lie,
Ye saw that the land lay fenceless, and ye let the months go by
Waiting some easy wonder, hoping some saving sign—
Idle—openly idle—in the lee of the forespent Line.
Idle—except for your boasting—and what is your boasting worth
If ye grudge a year of service to the lordliest life on earth?
Ancient, effortless, ordered, cycle on cycle set,
Life so long untroubled, that ye who inherit forget
It was not made with the mountains, it is not one with the deep.
Men, not gods, devised it. Men, not gods, must keep.
Men, not children, servants, or kinsfolk called from afar,
But each man born in the Island broke to the matter of war.
Soberly and by custom taken and trained for the same,
Each man born in the Island entered at youth to the game—

---

4. Untrained recruits London, who were called the City Imperial Volunteers.
5. Many of the gifts sent to the troops abroad were useless.
6. The Younger Nations included the British colonies of Australia, Canada, and New Zealand. The men from these nations were better prepared for the challenges of warfare.
7. The "flannelled fools" and "muddied oafs" were sportsmen playing cricket or football.

As it were almost cricket, not to be mastered in haste,
But after trial and labour, by temperance, living chaste.
As it were almost cricket—as it were even your play,
Weighed and pondered and worshipped, and practised day and day.
So ye shall bide sure-guarded when the restless lightnings wake
In the womb of the blotting war-cloud, and the pallid nations quake.
So, at the haggard trumpets, instant your soul shall leap
Forthright, accoutred, accepting—alert from the wells of sleep.
So, at the threat ye shall summon—so at the need ye shall send
Men, not children or servants, tempered and taught to the end;
Cleansed of servile panic, slow to dread or despise,
Humble because of knowledge, mighty by sacrifice. . . .
But ye say, "It will mar our comfort." Ye say, "It will minish our trade."
Do ye wait for the spattered shrapnel ere ye learn how a gun is laid?
For the low, red glare to southward when the raided coast-towns burn?
(Light ye shall have on that lesson, but little time to learn.)
Will ye pitch some white pavilion, and lustily even the odds,
With nets and hoops and mallets, with rackets and bats and rods
Will the rabbit war with your foemen—the red deer horn them for hire?
Your kept cock-pheasant keep you?—he is master of many a shire,
Arid, aloof, incurious, unthinking, unthanking, gelt,[8]
Will ye loose your schools to flout them till their brow-beat columns
   melt?
Will ye pray them or preach them, or print them, or ballot them back
   from your shore?
Will your workmen issue a mandate to bid them strike no more?
Will ye rise and dethrone your rulers? (Because ye were idle both?
Pride by Insolence chastened? Indolence purged by Sloth?)
No doubt but ye are the People; who shall make you afraid?
Also your gods are many; no doubt but your gods shall aid.
Idols of greasy altars built for the body's ease;
Proud little brazen Baals[9] and talking fetishes;
Teraphs of sept and party[10] and wise wood-pavement gods[11]—
These shall come down to the battle and snatch you from under the
   rods?

---

8. Deprived of vitality.
9. False gods worshiped in the Old Testament.
10. Petty gods worshiped by an insular clan.
11. Mocking those who made it a priority to pave the streets with wood.

From the gusty, flickering gun-roll with viewless salvoes rent,
And the pitted hail of the bullets that tell not whence they were sent.
When ye are ringed as with iron, when ye are scourged as with whips,
When the meat is yet in your belly, and the boast is yet on your lips;
When ye go forth at morning and the noon beholds you broke,
Ere ye lie down at even, your remnant, under the yoke?

No doubt but ye are the People—absolute, strong, and wise;
Whatever your heart has desired ye have not withheld from your eyes.
On your own heads, in your own hands, the sin and the saving lies!

THE PEACE OF DIVES

The Word came down to Dives[1] in Torment where he lay:
"Our World is full of wickedness, My Children maim and slay,
 And the Saint and Seer and Prophet
 Can make no better of it
Than to sanctify and prophesy and pray.

"Rise up, rise up, thou Dives, and take again thy gold,
And thy women and thy housen as they were to thee of old.
 It may be grace hath found thee
 In the furnace where We bound thee,
And that thou shalt bring the peace My Son foretold."

Then merrily rose Dives and leaped from out his fire,
And walked abroad with diligence to do the Lord's desire;
 And anon the battles ceased,
 And the captives were released,
And Earth had rest from Goshen to Gadire.[2]

The Word came down to Satan that raged and roared alone,
'Mid the shouting of the peoples by the cannon overthrown
 (But the Prophets, Saints, and Seers
 Set each other by the ears,
For each would claim the marvel as his own):

---

1. Dives represents a rich man who must learn to use his wealth in a way to benefit his fellowman. See Luke 16:19-31.
2. Goshen is the part of Egypt the Israelites inhabited while they were in bondage. Gadire is the country of the Gadarenes; it is found in the Galilee area of Israel.

"Rise up, rise up, thou Satan, upon the Earth to go,
And prove the Peace of Dives if it be good or no:
    For all that he hath planned
    We deliver to thy hand,
As thy skill shall serve, to break it or bring low."

Then mightily rose Satan, and about the Earth he hied,
And breathed on Kings in idleness and Princes drunk with pride;
    But for all the wrong he breathed
    There was never sword unsheathed,
And the fires he lighted flickered out and died.

Then terribly rose Satan, and darkened Earth afar,
Till he came on cunning Dives where the money-changers are;
    And he saw men pledge their gear
    For the gold that buys the spear,
And the helmet and the habergeon of war.

Yea, to Dives came the Persian and the Syrian and the Mede[3]—
And their hearts were nothing altered, nor their cunning nor their
greed—
    And they pledged their flocks and farms
    For the King-compelling arms,
And Dives lent according to their need.

Then Satan said to Dives:—"Return again with me,
Who hast broken His Commandment in the day He set thee free,
    Who grindest for thy greed
    Man's belly-pinch and need,
And the blood of Man to filthy usury!"

Then softly answered Dives where the money-changers sit:—
"My Refuge is Our Master, O My Master in the Pit.
    But behold all Earth is laid
    In the Peace which I have made,
And behold I wait on thee to trouble it!"

---

3. These are traditional enemies of the Jews (see, for example, Daniel 6:12), but they also have agreed to deal with Dives.

Then angrily turned Satan, and about the Seas he fled,
To shake the new-sown peoples with insult, doubt, and dread;
   But, for all the sleight he used,
   There was never squadron loosed,
And the brands he flung flew dying and fell dead.

But to Dives came Atlantis and the Captains of the West[4]—
And their hates were nothing weakened nor their anger nor unrest—
   And they pawned their utmost trade
   For the dry, decreeing blade;
And Dives lent and took of them their best.

Then Satan said to Dives:—"Declare thou by The Name,
The secret of thy subtlety that turneth mine to shame.
   It is known through all the Hells
   How my peoples mocked my spells,
And my faithless Kings denied me ere I came."

Then answered cunning Dives: "Do not gold and hate abide
At the heart of every Magic, yea, and senseless fear beside?
   With gold and fear and hate
   I have harnessed state to state,
And by hate and fear and gold their hates are tied.

"For hate men seek a weapon, for fear they seek a shield—
Keener blades and broader targes[5] than their frantic neighbours
wield—
   For gold I arm their hands,
   And for gold I buy their lands,
And for gold I sell their enemies the yield.

"Their nearest foes may purchase, or their furthest friends may lease,
One by one from Ancient Accad to the Islands of the Seas.[6]
   And their covenants they make
   For the naked iron's sake,
But I—I trap them armoured into peace.

---

4. This may have reference to the western hemisphere.
5. An archaic word for targets.
6. Accad was a principal city of the kingdom of Babylon (see also Genesis 10:10). For the Islands of the Sea, see Isaiah 11:11.

"The flocks that Egypt pledged me to Assyria I drave,
And Pharaoh hath the increase of the herds that Sargon[7] gave.
  Not for Ashdod[8] overthrown
  Will the Kings destroy their own,
Or their peoples wake the strife they feign to brave.

"Is not Carchemish like Calno?[9] For the steeds of their desire
They have sold me seven harvests that I sell to Crowning Tyre;[10]
  And the Tyrian sweeps the plains
  With a thousand hired wains,
And the Cities keep the peace and—share the hire.

"Hast thou seen the pride of Moab?[11] For the swords about his path,
His bond is to Philistia,[12] in half of all he hath.
  And he dare not draw the sword
  Till Gaza[13] give the word,
And he show release from Askalon and Gath.[14]

"Wilt thou call again thy peoples, wilt thou craze anew thy Kings?
Lo! my lightnings pass before thee, and their whistling servant brings,
  Ere the drowsy street hath stirred,
  Every masked and midnight word,
And the nations break their fast upon these things.

"So I make a jest of Wonder, and a mock of Time and Space,
The roofless Seas an hostel, and the Earth a market-place,
  Where the anxious traders know
  Each is surety for his foe,
And none may thrive without his fellows' grace.

"Now this is all my subtlety and this is all my wit,
God give thee good enlightenment, My Master in the Pit.
  But behold all Earth is laid
  In the Peace which I have made,
And behold I wait on thee to trouble it!"

---

7. A king of Assyria (see Isaiah 20:1).
8. A Philistine city (see 1 Samuel 5:1).
9. See Isaiah 10:7-9.
10. See Isaiah 23:8.
11. See Isaiah 16:6; Jeremiah 48:29.
12. The Philistines were longtime enemies of the people of Israel.
13. The greatest stronghold of the Philistines.
14. Cities on the eastern and western borders of Philistia.

THE SETTLER

(South African War ended, May, 1902)

Here, where my fresh-turned furrows run,
  And the deep soil glistens red,
I will repair the wrong that was done
  To the living and the dead.
Here, where the senseless bullet fell,
  And the barren shrapnel burst,
I will plant a tree, I will dig a well,
  Against the heat and the thirst.

Here, in a large and a sunlit land,
  Where no wrong bites to the bone,
I will lay my hand in my neighbour's hand,
  And together we will atone
For the set folly and the red breach
  And the black waste of it all;
Giving and taking counsel each
  Over the cattle-kraal.[1]

Here will we join against our foes—
  The hailstroke and the storm,
And the red and rustling cloud that blows
  The locust's mile-deep swarm.
Frost and murrain and floods let loose
  Shall launch us side by side
In the holy wars that have no truce
  'Twixt seed and harvest-tide.

---

1. Corral.

Earth, where we rode to slay or be slain,
   Our love shall redeem unto life.
We will gather and lead to her lips again
   The waters of ancient strife,
From the far and fiercely guarded streams
   And the pools where we lay in wait,
Till the corn cover our evil dreams
   And the young corn our hate.

And when we bring old fights to mind,
   We will not remember the sin—
If there be blood on his head of my kind,
   Or blood on my head of his kin—
For the ungrazed upland, the untilled lea
   Cry, and the fields forlorn:
"The dead must bury their dead,[2] but ye—
   Ye serve an host unborn."

Bless then, Our God, the new-yoked plough
   And the good beasts that draw,
And the bread we eat in the sweat of our brow[3]
   According to Thy Law.
After us cometh a multitude—
   Prosper the work of our hands,
That we may feed with our land's food
   The folk of all our lands!

Here, in the waves and the troughs of the plains,
   Where the healing stillness lies,
And the vast, benignant sky restrains
   And the long days make wise—
Bless to our use the rain and the sun
   And the blind seed in its bed,
That we may repair the wrong that was done
   To the living and the dead!

---

2. See Luke 9:59-62.
3. See Genesis 3:19.

THE QUESTION

"Neutrals"[1]

Brethren, how shall it fare with me
  When the war is laid aside,
If it be proven that I am he
  For whom a world has died?

If it be proven that all my good,
  And the greater good I will make,
Were purchased me by a multitude
  Who suffered for my sake?

That I was delivered by mere mankind
  Vowed to one sacrifice,
And not, as I hold them, battle-blind,
  But dying with open eyes?

That they did not ask me to draw the sword
  When they stood to endure their lot—
That they only looked to me for a word,
  And I answered I knew them not?

---

1. This poem was written in 1916, when bitterness was high in Britain that U.S. President Woodrow Wilson was maintaining neutrality in World War I. It was originally titled "The Neutral." When the poem was reprinted in 1929, Kipling made "Neutrals" the subtitle, and in a 1933 reprinting he added the explanatory note, "Attitude of the United States of America during the first two years, seven months, and four days of the Great War."

If it be found, when the battle clears,
  Their death has set me free,
Then how shall I live with myself through the years
  Which they have bought for me?

Brethren, how must it fare with me,
  Or how am I justified,
If it be proven that I am he
  For whom mankind has died—
If it be proven that I am he
  Who, being questioned, denied?

A NATIVITY

The Babe was laid in the Manger
Between the gentle kine—
All safe from cold and danger—
"But it was not so with mine,
        (With mine! With mine!)
"Is it well with the child, is it well?"[1]
The waiting mother prayed.
"For I know not how he fell,
And I know not where he is laid."

A Star stood forth in Heaven;
The Watchers ran to see
The Sign of the Promise given—
"But there comes no sign to me.
        (To me! To me!)
"*My* child died in the dark.
Is it well with the child, is it well?
There was none to tend him or mark,
And I know not how he fell."

The Cross was raised on high;
The Mother grieved beside—
"But the Mother saw Him die
And took Him when He died.
        (He died! He died!)

---

1. See 2 Kings 4:26.

160

"Seemly and undefiled
    His burial-place was made—
Is it well, is it well with the child?
    For I know not where he is laid."

On the dawning of Easter Day
    Comes Mary Magdalene;
But the Stone was rolled away,
    And the Body was not within—
        (Within! Within!)
"Ah, who will answer my word?
    The broken mother prayed.
"They have taken away my Lord,
    And I know not where He is laid."

                    ***

The Star stands forth in Heaven.
    The watchers watch in vain
For Sign of the Promise given
    Of peace on Earth again—
        (Again! Again!)
"But I know for Whom he fell"—
    The steadfast mother smiled,
"Is it well with the child—is it well?
    It is well—it is well with the child!"

THE BEGINNINGS

It was not part of their blood,
  It came to them very late
With long arrears to make good,
  When the English began to hate.

They were not easily moved,
  They were icy-willing to wait
Till every count should be proved,
  Ere the English began to hate.

Their voices were even and low,
  Their eyes were level and straight.
There was neither sign nor show,
  When the English began to hate.

It was not preached to the crowd,
  It was not taught by the State.
No man spoke it aloud,
  When the English began to hate.

It was not suddenly bred,
  It will not swiftly abate,
Through the chill years ahead,
  When Time shall count from the date
  That the English began to hate.

THE OUTLAWS

Through learned and laborious years
  They set themselves to find
Fresh terrors and undreamed-of fears
  To heap upon mankind.

All that they drew from Heaven above
  Or digged from earth beneath,
They laid into their treasure-trove
  And arsenals of death:

While, for well-weighed advantage sake,
  Ruler and ruled alike
Built up the faith they meant to break
  When the fit hour should strike.

They traded with the careless earth,
  And good return it gave:
They plotted by their neighbour's hearth
  The means to make him slave.

When all was ready to their hand
  They loosed their hidden sword,
And utterly laid waste a land
  Their oath was pledged to guard.

Coldly they went about to raise
  To life and make more dread
Abominations of old days,
  That men believed were dead.

They paid the price to reach their goal
  Across a world in flame;
But their own hate slew their own soul
  Before that victory came.

THE CHILDREN

These were our children who died for our lands: they were dear in
   our sight.[1]
We have only the memory left of their home-treasured sayings and
   laughter.
The price of our loss shall be paid to our hands, not another's
   hereafter.
Neither the Alien nor Priest shall decide on it.   That is our right.
But who shall return us the children?[2]

At the hour the Barbarian chose to disclose his pretences,
   And raged against Man, they engaged, on the breasts that they
      bared for us,
   The first felon-stroke of the sword he had long-time prepared for us—
Their bodies were all our defence while we wrought our defences.

They bought us anew with their blood, forbearing to blame us,
Those hours which we had not made good when the Judgment o'ercame
   us.
They believed us and perished for it.   Our statecraft, our learning
Delivered them bound to the Pit and alive to the burning
Whither they mirthfully hastened as jostling for honour.
Not since her birth has our Earth seen such worth loosed upon her.

---

1. Much of this poem lacks the polished rhythm typical of Kipling. The tone, sometimes
choppy and even conversational, underscores the raw feelings of the bereaved parents
who are speaking the lines.
   2. This poem was written after World War I had been raging for three years. During
that war, nearly 1 million British soldiers were killed and another 2 million were wounded.
Rudyard Kipling's only son, John, was among the dead, having been killed at the Battle
of Loos in 1915. The sting of John's loss was sharpened by the fact that Rudyard had
pulled strings to help his near-sighted son enlist.

Nor was their agony brief, or once only imposed on them.
  The wounded, the war-spent, the sick received no exemption:
  Being cured they returned and endured and achieved our
      redemption,
Hopeless themselves of relief, till Death, marvelling, closed on them.

That flesh we had nursed from the first in all cleanness was given
To corruption unveiled and assailed by the malice of Heaven—
By the heart-shaking jests of Decay where it lolled on the wires—
To be blanched or gay-painted by fumes—to be cindered by fires—
To be senselessly tossed and retossed in stale mutilation
From crater to crater.   For this we shall take expiation.
    But who shall return us our children?

MESOPOTAMIA

They shall not return to us, the resolute, the young,[1]
The eager and whole-hearted whom we gave:
But the men who left them thriftily to die in their own dung,
Shall they come with years and honour to the grave?

They shall not return to us; the strong men coldly slain
In sight of help denied from day to day:
But the men who edged their agonies and chid them in their pain,
Are they too strong and wise to put away?

Our dead shall not return to us while Day and Night divide—
Never while the bars of sunset hold.
But the idle-minded overlings who quibbled while they died,
Shall they thrust for high employments as of old?

Shall we only threaten and be angry for an hour:
When the storm is ended shall we find
How softly but how swiftly they have sidled back to power
By the favour and contrivance of their kind?

Even while they soothe us, while they promise large amends,
Even while they make a show of fear,
Do they call upon their debtors, and take counsel with their friends,
To conform and reestablish each career?

---

1. This poem was written in response to the disastrous British campaign in the Middle
East during World War I. The campaign marked by incompetence and unwise decisions
that resulted in many deaths, but those responsible continued in their careers without
consequence.

Their lives cannot repay us—their death could not undo—
   The shame that they have laid upon our race.
But the slothfulness that wasted and the arrogance that slew,
   Shall we leave it unabated in its place?

JUSTICE

Across a world where all men grieve
  And grieving strive the more,
The great days range like tides and leave
  Our dead on every shore.
Heavy the load we undergo,
  And our own hands prepare,
If we have parley with the foe,
  The load our sons must bear.

Before we loose the word
  That bids new worlds to birth,
Needs must we loosen first the sword
  Of Justice upon earth;
Or else all else is vain
  Since life on earth began,
And the spent world sinks back again
  Hopeless of God and Man.

A People and their King
  Through ancient sin grown strong,
Because they feared no reckoning
  Would set no bound to wrong;
But now their hour is past,
  And we who bore it find
Evil Incarnate hell at last
  To answer to mankind.

For agony and spoil
  Of nations beat to dust,
For poisoned air and tortured soil
  And cold, commanded lust,
And every secret woe
  The shuddering waters saw—
Willed and fulfilled by high and low—
  Let them relearn the Law:

That when the dooms are read,
  Not high nor low shall say:—
"My haughty or my humble head
  Has saved me in this day."
That, till the end of time,
  Their remnant shall recall
Their fathers' old, confederate crime
  Availed them not at all:

That neither schools nor priests,
  Nor Kings may build again
A people with the heart of beasts
  Made wise concerning men.
Whereby our dead shall sleep
  In honour, unbetrayed,
And we in faith and honour keep
  That peace for which they paid.

RUSSIA TO THE PACIFISTS

God rest you, peaceful gentlemen, let nothing you dismay,
But—leave your sports a little while—the dead are borne this way!
Armies dead and Cities dead, past all count or care.
God rest you, merry gentlemen, what portent see you there?
    Singing:—Break ground for a wearied host
    That have no ground to keep.
    Give them the rest that they covet most . . .
    And who shall next to sleep, good sirs,
    In such a trench to sleep?

God rest you, peaceful gentlemen, but give us leave to pass.
We go to dig a nation's grave as great as England was.
For this Kingdom and this Glory and this Power and this Pride
Three hundred years it flourished—in three hundred days it died.
    Singing:—Pour oil for a frozen throng,
    That lie about the ways.
    Give them the warmth they have lacked so long . . .
    And what shall be next to blaze, good sirs,
    On such a pyre to blaze?

God rest you, thoughtful gentlemen, and send your sleep is light!
Remains of this dominion no shadow, sound, or sight,
Except the sound of weeping and the sight of burning fire,
And the shadow of a people that is trampled into mire.
    Singing:—Break bread for a starving folk
    That perish in the field.
    Give them their food as they take the yoke . . .
    And who shall be next to yield, good sirs,
    For such a bribe to yield?

God rest you merry gentlemen, and keep you in your mirth!
Was ever Kingdom turned so soon to ashes, blood and earth?
'Twixt the summer and the snow-seeding-time and frost—
Arms and victual, hope and counsel, name and country lost!
    Singing:—*Let down by the foot and the head—*
      Shovel and smooth it all!
      So do we bury a Nation dead . . .
      And who shall be next to fall, good sirs,
      With your good help to fall?

THE HYAENAS

After the burial-parties leave
  And the baffled kites have fled;
The wise hyaenas come out at eve
  To take account of our dead.

How he died and why he died
  Troubles them not a whit.
They snout the bushes and stones aside
  And dig till they come to it.

They are only resolute they shall eat
  That they and their mates may thrive,
And they know that the dead are safer meat
  Than the weakest thing alive.

(For a goat may butt, and a worm may sting,
  And a child will sometimes stand;
But a poor dead soldier of the King
  Can never lift a hand.)

They whoop and halloo and scatter the dirt
  Until their tushes white[1]
Take good hold in the army shirt,
  And tug the corpse to light,

---

1. Long, sharp teeth.

And the pitiful face is shewn again
  For an instant ere they close;
But it is not discovered to living men—
  Only to God and to those

Who, being soulless, are free from shame,
  Whatever meat they may find.
Nor do they defile the dead man's name—
  That is reserved for his kind.

THE TRUCE OF THE BEAR

Yearly, with tent and rifle, our careless white men go
By the Pass called Muttianee, to shoot in the vale below.
Yearly by Muttianee he follows our white men in—
Matun, the old blind beggar, bandaged from brow to chin.

Eyeless, noseless, and lipless—toothless, broken of speech,
Seeking a dole at the doorway he mumbles his tale to each;
Over and over the story, ending as he began:
"Make ye no truce with Adam-zad—the Bear that walks like a Man!

"There was a flint in my musket—pricked and primed was the pan,
When I went hunting Adam-zad—the Bear that stands like a Man.
I looked my last on the timber, I looked my last on the snow,
When I went hunting Adam-zad fifty summers ago!

"I knew his times and his seasons, as he knew mine, that fed
By night in the ripened maizefield and robbed my house of bread.
I knew his strength and cunning, as he knew mine, that crept
At dawn to the crowded goat-pens and plundered while I slept.

"Up from his stony playground—down from his well-digged lair—
Out on the naked ridges ran Adam-zad the Bear—
Groaning, grunting, and roaring, heavy with stolen meals,
Two long marches to northward, and I was at his heels!

"Two long marches to northward, at the fall of the second night,
I came on mine enemy Adam-zad all panting from his flight.
There was a charge in the musket—pricked and primed was the pan—
My finger crooked on the trigger—when he reared up like a man.

174

"Horrible, hairy, human, with paws like hands in prayer,
Making his supplication rose Adam-zad the Bear!
I looked at the swaying shoulders, at the paunch's swag and swing,
And my heart was touched with pity for the monstrous, pleading thing.

"Touched with pity and wonder, I did not fire then . . .
I have looked no more on women—I have walked no more with men.
Nearer he tottered and nearer, with paws like hands that pray—
From brow to jaw that steel-shod paw, it ripped my face away!

"Sudden, silent, and savage, searing as flame the blow—
Faceless I fell before his feet, fifty summers ago.
I heard him grunt and chuckle—I heard him pass to his den.
He left me blind to the darkened years and the little mercy of men.

"Now ye go down in the morning with guns of the newer style,
That load (I have felt) in the middle and range (I have heard) a mile?
Luck to the white man's rifle, that shoots so fast and true,
But—pay, and I lift my bandage and show what the Bear can do!"

(Flesh like slag in the furnace, knobbed and withered and grey—
Matun, the old blind beggar, he gives good worth for his pay.)
"Rouse him at noon in the bushes, follow and press him hard—
Not for his ragings and roarings flinch ye from Adam-zad.

"But (pay, and I put back the bandage) *this* is the time to fear,
When he stands up like a tired man, tottering near and near;
When he stands up as pleading, in wavering, man-brute guise,
When he veils the hate and cunning of his little, swinish eyes;

"When he shows as seeking quarter, with paws like hands in prayer
That is the time of peril—the time of the Truce of the Bear!"

Eyeless, noseless, and lipless, asking a dole at the door,
Matun, the old blind beggar, he tells it o'er and o'er;
Fumbling and feeling the rifles, warming his hands at the flame,
Hearing our careless white men talk of the morrow's game;

Over and over the story, ending as he began:—
"There is no truce with Adam-zad, the Bear that looks like a Man!"

THE BENEFACTORS

Ah! What avails the classic bent
  And what the cultured word,
Against the undoctored incident
  That actually occurred?

And what is Art whereto we press
  Through paint and prose and rhyme—
When Nature in her nakedness
  Defeats us every time?

It is not learning, grace nor gear,
  Nor easy meat and drink,
But bitter pinch of pain and fear
  That makes creation think.

When in this world's unpleasing youth
  Our godlike race began,
The longest arm, the sharpest tooth,
  Gave man control of man;

Till, bruised and bitten to the bone
  And taught by pain and fear,
He learned to deal the far-off stone,
  And poke the long, safe spear.

So tooth and nail were obsolete
  As means against a foe,
Till, bored by uniform defeat,
  Some genius built the bow.

Then stone and javelin proved as vain
  As old-time tooth and nail;
Till, spurred anew by fear and pain,
  Man fashioned coats of mail.

Then was there safety for the rich
  And danger for the poor,
Till someone mixed a powder which
  Redressed the scale once more.

Helmet and armour disappeared
  With sword and bow and pike,
And, when the smoke of battle cleared,
  All men were armed alike. . . .

And when ten million such were slain
  To please one crazy king,
Man, schooled in bulk by fear and pain,
  Grew weary of the thing;

And, at the very hour designed,
  To enslave him past recall,
His tooth-stone-arrow-gun-shy mind
  Turned and abolished all.

All Power, each Tyrant, every Mob
  Whose head has grown too large,
Ends by destroying its own job
  And works its own discharge;

And Man, whose mere necessities
  Move all things from his path,
Trembles meanwhile at their decrees,
  And deprecates their wrath!

GETHSEMANE

The Garden called Gethsemane[1]
  In Picardy[2] it was,
And there the people came to see
  The English soldiers pass.
We used to pass—we used to pass
  Or halt, as it might be,
And ship our masks in case of gas
  Beyond Gethsemane.

The Garden called Gethsemane,
  It held a pretty lass,
But all the time she talked to me
  I prayed my cup might pass.
The officer sat on the chair,
  The men lay on the grass,
And all the time we halted there
  I prayed my cup might pass.

It didn't pass—it didn't pass—
  It didn't pass from me.
I drank it when we met the gas
  Beyond Gethsemane!

---

1. The location where Jesus prayed on the night before he was crucified. See Matthew 26:36-46.
2. A province in the north of France.

EPITAPHS OF WAR (EXCERPTS)

AN ONLY SON
I have slain none except my Mother. She
(Blessing her slayer) died of grief for me.

THE WONDER
Body and Spirit I surrendered whole
To harsh Instructors—and received a soul . . .
If mortal man could change me through and through
From all I was—what may The God not do?

SHOCK
My name, my speech, my self I had forgot.
My wife and children came—I knew them not.
I died. My Mother followed. At her call
And on her bosom I remembered all.

COMMON FORM
If any question why we died,
Tell them, because our fathers lied.

A DEAD STATESMAN
I could not dig: I dared not rob:
Therefore I lied to please the mob.
Now all my lies are proved untrue
And I must face the men I slew.
What tale shall serve me here among
Mine angry and defrauded young?

THE REBEL
If I had clamoured at Thy Gate
  For gift of Life on Earth,
And, thrusting through the souls that wait,
  Flung headlong into birth—
Even then, even then, for gin and snare
  About my pathway spread,
Lord, I had mocked Thy thoughtful care
  Before I joined the Dead!
But now? . . . I was beneath Thy Hand
  Ere yet the Planets came.
And now—though Planets pass, I stand
  The witness to Thy shame!

THE OBEDIENT
Daily, though no ears attended,
  Did my prayers arise.
Daily, though no fire descended,
  Did I sacrifice.
Though my darkness did not lift,
  Though I faced no lighter odds,
Though the Gods bestowed no gift,
      None the less,
  None the less, I served the Gods!

UNKNOWN FEMALE CORPSE
Headless, lacking foot and hand,
Horrible I come to land.
I beseech all women's sons
Know I was a mother once.

RAPED AND REVENGED
One used and butchered me: another spied
Me broken—for which thing an hundred died.
So it was learned among the heathen hosts
How much a freeborn woman's favour costs.

THE BRIDEGROOM
Call me not false, beloved,
　If, from thy scarce-known breast
So little time removed,
　In other arms I rest.

For this more ancient bride,
　Whom coldly I embrace,
Was constant at my side
　Before I saw thy face.

Our marriage, often set—
　By miracle delayed—
At last is consummate,
　And cannot be unmade.

Live, then, whom Life shall cure,
　Almost, of Memory,
And leave us to endure
　Its immortality.

OLD FIGHTING-MEN

All the world over, nursing their scars,
Sit the old fighting-men broke in the wars—
Sit the old fighting-men, surly and grim
Mocking the lilt of the conquerors' hymn.

Dust of the battle o'erwhelmed them and hid.
Fame never found them for aught that they did.
Wounded and spent to the lazar they drew,
Lining the road where the Legions roll through.

Sons of the Laurel who press to your meed,
(Worthy God's pity most—you who succeed!)
Ere you go triumphing, crowned, to the stars,
Pity poor fighting-men, broke in the wars!

Part VI

EPILOGUE

WHEN EARTH'S LAST PICTURE IS PAINTED

When Earth's last picture is painted and the tubes are twisted and dried,
When the oldest colours have faded, and the youngest critic has died,
We shall rest, and, faith, we shall need it—lie down for an aeon or two,
Till the Master of All Good Workmen shall put us to work anew.

And those that were good shall be happy; they shall sit in a golden chair;
They shall splash at a ten-league canvas with brushes of comets' hair.
They shall find real saints to draw from—Magdalene, Peter, and Paul;
They shall work for an age at a sitting and never be tired at all!

And only The Master shall praise us, and only The Master shall blame;
And no one shall work for money, and no one shall work for fame,
But each for the joy of the working, and each, in his separate star,
Shall draw the Thing as he sees It for the God of Things as They are!